What Christian leaders are saying about <u>Jesus, Man of Joy</u> . . .

"Dr. Wirt is on to something great and marvelous! When he tells us that joy in God, under God, as a gift from God, is the heart of Christianity, he is right—and we need the reminder. Come one, come all, and learn the joy of exploring joy with Sherwood Wirt."

J. I. Packer

"A lovely tribute to the most important person ever to walk this earth—the Son of God, our Lord Jesus Christ. Sherwood Wirt refreshingly captures anew the magnificence of this One whom the apostle John calls 'The Word made flesh.' He helps one fall even more in love with the One altogether lovely, full of joy."

Ted W. Engstrom

"Dr. Wirt asks and answers the haunting question of contemporary Christianity: 'Where did we churchfolk lose out? How did we drift so far from the joy of the Lord?' [This book] brought me to a refreshing renewal of joy . . . "

Lloyd John Ogilvie

"what a refreshing word for our day . . . joy! i was particularly impressed with the scriptural insights showing clearly the source of cosmic joy . . . the very character of our Almighty God. these chapters have given me a refreshed perspective on life . . . radiant joy is always possible! Jesus never fails. it pays to serve Him."

ann kiemel anderson

"In the pressures of life we usually tend to one of two extremes—to be over-serious, or to drug ourselves in entertainment. There is another option—joy—a quality of life with its roots in God. This is the quality my friend, Sherwood Wirt, lifts up in his refreshing new book."

Leighton Ford

"Dr. Wirt has not only written an excellent book on joy, but he has done it in a way that makes reading it a joyful experience!"

Warren W. Wiersbe

"Sherwood Wirt has blessed so many for so long it's unsurprising that we should continue to find wisdom and joy for our souls flowing from his pen."

Jack Hayford

"An extraordinarily refreshing book brimming with the joy Jesus expressed . . . and wants His followers to share. Dr. Wirt skillfully debunks the myth that Christianity represents a sober-sided approach to life. And he is one of the best examples I know of the joy of Jesus."
Josh McDowell

"Sherwood Wirt first touched my life with his writings when I was a college student more than a quarter of a century ago. God continues to communicate marvelous truth through him in a most refreshing and edifying manner. This volume has got to be one of his best—coming from his heart and life!"
Paul A. Cedar

"For more than 50 years Jesus has been for me the secret, the source, and the strength of my joy. *Jesus, Man of Joy,* this marvelous book by Sherwood E. Wirt, has given me fresh insight and understanding as to the 'why' and the 'how' of this wonderful truth."
Cliff Barrows

"Sherwood Wirt has walked a long time with Christ. To know him is to sense the fullness of affection for his Lord. I always find it easy to trust the wisdom of a man who never trusts his own wisdom. So may you read this book as you would read a life that binds you to itself with an authority never asked for, but conferred because of faithfulness. In these pages are the over-spillings of a deep cup."
Calvin Miller

"Far too many Christians equate spirituality with a long face and misery—as though God were a killjoy. In my preaching, teaching and writing I have often stressed that those who know Christ as Savior and Lord should be the most joyful people in the world (Philippians 4:4). Sherwood Wirt has helped us recapture that significant truth. Read this book and celebrate Jesus' joy—experience it for yourself (John 15:11)."
Kenneth L. Barker

"Joy is the badge of a person in touch with the living God. For centuries, Christians have been crippled in their walk with God because of a lack of the spiritual fruit of joy! Dr. Wirt is a man overflowing with joy, and in my eyes, more than qualified to write on the subject."
Mike MacIntosh

"This book is powerful medicine for those who are sick and depressed—and for those who think frowning is holy."
Jamie Buckingham

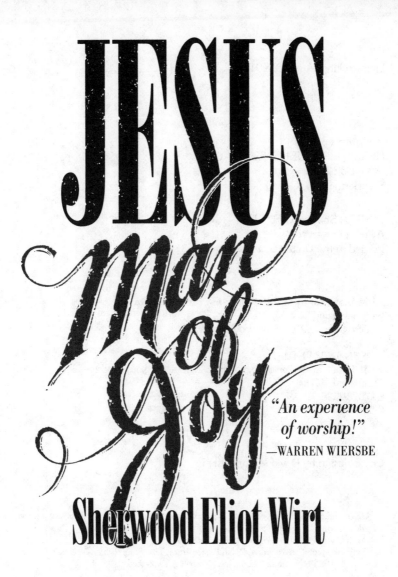

JESUS
Man of Joy

"An experience
of worship!"
—WARREN WIERSBE

Sherwood Eliot Wirt

Here's Life Publishers

First Printing, August 1991

Published by
HERE'S LIFE PUBLISHERS, INC.
P. O. Box 1576
San Bernardino, CA 92402

Library of Congress Cataloging-in-Publication Data
Wirt, Sherwood Eliot.
   Jesus, man of joy / Sherwood Eliot Wirt.
      p.   cm.
   ISBN 0-89840-319-7
   1. Jesus Christ—Person and offices. 2. Joy—Religious aspects—
Christianity. I. Title.
BT202.W595   1991   91-628
232.9'04—dc20   CIP

Cover design by David Marty Design

Unless indicated otherwise, Scripture quotations are from *The Holy Bible: New International Version,* © 1973, 1978, 1984 by the International Bible Society. Published by Zondervan Bible Publishers, Grand Rapids, Michigan.

Scripture quotations designated NKJV are from *The Holy Bible: New King James Version,* © 1982 by Thomas Nelson, Inc., Nashville, Tennessee.

For More Information, Write:
L.I.F.E.—P.O. Box A399, Sydney South 2000, Australia
Campus Crusade for Christ of Canada—Box 300, Vancouver, B.C., V6C 2X3, Canada
Campus Crusade for Christ—Pearl Assurance House, 4 Temple Row, Birmingham, B2 5HG, England
Lay Institute for Evangelism—P.O. Box 8786, Auckland 3, New Zealand
Campus Crusade for Christ—P.O. Box 240, Raffles City Post Office, Singapore 9117
Great Commission Movement of Nigeria—P.O. Box 500, Jos, Plateau State Nigeria, West Africa
Campus Crusade for Christ International—Arrowhead Springs, San Bernardino, CA 92414, U.S.A.

*To the memory of
my mother and father*

Contents

Foreword

We all have our heroes and heroines. They are historical characters or contemporary models who inspire our lives, constantly calling us to venture on in the pursuit of excellence. I have mine: preachers who exemplify that rare combination of profound biblical exposition and vivid illustration, and writers who set benchmarks for communicating eternal truth with fresh contemporary application in an impelling style, coupled with penetrating insight.

Sherwood Wirt has been one of my literary heroes. During the past twenty-five years, as I have tried to put my convictions and vision into words for publication, Dr. Wirt's books have been both a model and an inspiration.

But "Woody" (as his friends affectionately call him) is not only a writer's writer, he is also a reader's writer. His impeccable rhetoric dances and sings and calls his readers to think magnificently about God and then to kneel on the knees of their hearts. For good reason: Wirt blends in-depth understanding of the Scriptures, theological wisdom, a vital evangelical faith, rich mining of classical and contemporary literature, and moving real-life stories in each of his "can't put it down" books. From his disciplined scholar's mind and his Spirit-filled disciple's heart flow his prayerfully ordered thoughts and anointed phrases. He is a master of the metaphor, a wordsmith who makes you want to underline and add some exclamation points of your own.

Sherwood Wirt's books have had such a lasting value because he has an uncanny way of putting his finger on the raw nerve in Christians and in the church. He lives on the creative edge of the spiritual adventure and winsomely invites us to share the exciting discoveries he is making.

This is especially true of the book you are about to read. You are in for a fresh experience of authentic joy. I know you will sense, as I did, that this book was written by a person who has been touched by a new burst of the ebullient joy, and he communicates that joy forcefully.

Unlike so many books that have attempted to explain joy, this one is wonderfully free of "oughts." Instead of telling us we ought to have joy by trying harder or straining to look or act joyfully, Wirt traces true joy right back to the nature of God, and he convincingly helps us to understand joy as an attribute of God. He puts our minds and hearts on tiptoe as he deftly leads us to the joy of God before time and creation. We feel the pulse-beat of this pre-existent joy, and then sense the outreaching of pure joy in the creation of universes within universes and humankind on the planet Earth, made by joy and for joy.

Then, while we are still breathless over the joy-motivated wonder of creation, we are introduced to a stunning portrait of Jesus that's often lost in our religious gallery of images of Him. The title of this book aptly describes this overlooked portrait—*Jesus, Man of Joy.*

And, as we are magnetically drawn from page to page of Wirt's word-portrait, we are able to picture the radiance of Jesus' joy and feel the palpable delight of His life. With "you are there" intensity, we live in the skins of the new breed of humanity called the early Christians, who realized Jesus' promise that His joy would be in them and their joy would be full.

Also, the author does not leave contemporary application to a postscript. Rather, at each stage of his explanation of joy, he spells out the implications for our life today. This prompts us to agree with Robert Louis Stevenson: "To miss the joy is to miss everything." Wirt helps us not to miss the joy by graciously leading us through the crucial steps of experiencing Jesus' joy now.

Nothing is more needed today. Joy is the missing ingredient in contemporary Christianity and in so many Christians. The author exposes our powerless piousness and grim religiosity. He is on target when he says, "The problem is the pseudo-religious smog that we spread over our church life, the unnecessary gravity with which our leadership protects its dignity, the unnatural churchly posturing that so easily passes into overbearing arrogance and conceit." Wirt cuts through this smog and vividly describes how the "radiant, overflowing inner joy that Jesus brought to earth and shared with His followers" can be the experience of Christians today. What's more, he shows us how the church can become a center of contagious joy to match the spiritual hunger and longing for authentic power openly expressed by the secular American today.

Dr. Wirt asks and answers the haunting questions of contemporary Christianity: "Where did we churchfolk lose out? How did we drift so far from the joy of the Lord? Does it not seem strange to you that we should be cut off—amputated—from the hope of the very thing that brought us to the church in the first place?" Yes, it is strange and alarming, especially when you catch the impact of the exhilarating elixir of Jesus' joy described in this book. How to be regrafted and receive the artesian flow of this joy is the book's thrilling thrust. It brought me to a refreshing renewal of joy; I pray for nothing less for you.

The billboard advertisements for Joy perfume say, "One whiff of Joy will make a rich man a generous man." This book is more than a whiff of scent—it's an experience of real joy that will transform your life!

Lloyd John Ogilvie

Acknowledgments

The apostle Paul wrote to the church at Galatia that his gospel was not the result of his "conferring with flesh and blood." I might dare to claim the same for the basic theme of this book, were I not continually in debt to the insights of my teachers, friends, relatives, editors, pastors, writing colleagues, and the whole corpus of Christian literature, past and present.

Especially I would like to recognize the help given me by Leslie Stobbe, Daniel Benson and Jean Bryant, my editors at Here's Life Publishers; by my wife Ruth, whose counsel has been invaluable; by certain writing friends in San Diego County; and by a host of people who responded positively to my expression that Jesus was a Man of Joy.

S.E.W.
Poway, California

1

The Secret

"Maybe we yearn to . . . rise above this banal, animalistic, low-grade, diminished cockroach level." —Lily Tomlin

*T*wo thousand years ago there appeared on this planet a Person who brought about an astonishing change in the quality of life among human beings. Whatever it was this Person had, it was unique. It set Him apart and made Him utterly fascinating to others. For a few brief years He was seen in the villages and towns of Palestine, which at the time were under Roman occupation. Then He disappeared, although some of His close followers claimed they had reason to believe He was—and is—still around.

From a strictly materialistic viewpoint, this Person's active life did not accomplish all that much. Remarkable actions were attributed to Him, but He wrote no epics and raised no monuments. In early youth He seems to have worked with His hands. Later He taught, prayed, and healed, as many prophets had done before Him and have done since. That He had noble character and personal charm, and uttered many wise things that people have been quoting ever since, could be said also of others.

Yet for this Person to be endowed with such universal appeal, there must have been something very special about Him. The world has never forgotten Him. His name is on someone's lips every second of time; in fact, time is dated from His birth. A billion human beings today claim to be His followers, and most of them are convinced that He is the Author of their personal salvation.

But if there was "something special" about Him, what was it? Chesterton tells us it was that He had a secret.

And what was this secret? I believe you will find it in the pages that follow. It has been divulged before, but still many appear not to have found it. Even among some of those who have risen to high eminence in His service it is still, tragically, a secret. Some people are known to live earnest and godly lives. They perform wonderful deeds and achieve mighty goals that bring abundant blessings to the human race. It seems inexplicable that they should miss the secret, but the fact is, they do.

What makes it so strange is that it is an open secret, spread on the pages of the New Testament for everyone to read. It may not be spelled out on every page, for a very good reason; and yet its effect can be felt all through the twenty-seven books and letters. It's a secret that explains, more than anything else could, the grip that this Person has held upon the lives of ordinary mankind and wom- ankind for these two millennia. It also helps to explain what

God had in mind when He created the universe and placed humans in it.

You probably have had the experience of looking at a painting and failing to notice something. Then someone in the room, who was also looking at the painting, pointed it out. Once you saw it, the picture took on an entirely new significance for you. That is the purpose of this book, to point out to you what you may have missed.

Millions of human beings today are going through a very hard time. They know something is wrong. Instinct tells them there is something better for them than what they are having to put up with, but they seem helpless to attain it.

> Thou madest man, he knows not why,
> He thinks he was not made to die.[1]

Lily Tomlin, the television comedienne who rose to television fame through her unforgettable portrayal of Ernestine in "Laugh-in," made this statement in a 1990 interview that appeared in the *San Francisco Chronicle:* "In a world where so many things are brutalizing and desensitizing, maybe we yearn to make something that fills us with a kind of elation, a sense of something joyful or lovely, a sense of inspiration. Anything to make us rise above this banal, animalistic, low-grade, diminished, cockroach level."[2]

I do not pretend to possess any special credentials or qualifications for this effort to "make something." Good heavens! Of what use are credentials when one is writing about the mind of the One who operates the cosmos? You may be certain that I have discovered nothing. The secret has been there all the time, and some have found it, while many haven't. It has no direct effect on our standing with

God, or our salvation or sanctification or glorification; but it has a lot to do with how we enjoy them all.

Would you like to know the secret?

Read on.

2

Cosmic Joy

What we see
through the giant telescopes
is an expression of joy by the Creator.

The secret of Jesus was—and is—His inner joy. Many intimations in the New Testament lead us to believe that while in our midst our Lord had a merry heart. To cite just one statement in the Gospel of Luke: "At that time Jesus, full of joy through the Holy Spirit, said, 'I praise You, Father.'"[1]

Where did this exuberant disposition come from? On the human side, of course, from his mother Mary. Is anything in the Bible more beautiful than Luke's story of the first Christmas when the joy of the angels filled the air above Bethlehem? Mary was a true daughter of the Hebrew race which has always been known for its joyous and sunny spirit. To this the Old Testament bears witness, for it contains more than inspired teaching, history and prophecy; it is also the record of a people's songs and celebrations.

But there was a second, far more profound supernatural source of Jesus' inner joy. It came from Heaven, which is the original seat of all joy. (Where else could it have come from?) The Gospel of Luke tells us that before Mary was married to Joseph, the angel Gabriel paid her a visit. He informed her that the Holy Spirit would come upon her, and the power of the Most High would overshadow her. Matthew says the angel told Joseph that Mary would give birth to a Son, and Joseph was to name Him Jesus, because He would save His people from their sins.[2] This Son would not have a human father. He would be called the Son of God.

Later in the unfolding of Scripture He would be recognized as the Second Person of the Godhead, the Logos or Word who was in the beginning with God. Such profound theological concepts are not easily grasped by the mind. Even when we are eager to accept them, they drift beyond us. To take them in, in order that we might look for the true source of the joy in Jesus' life, it becomes necessary to go back—not to the first century, not to the antediluvian or Mesozoic or Paleozoic eras, or even to the beginning of time itself, but farther back—into eternity.

Let me invite you to step out on the patio of our modest home for a moment. It is a clear, beautiful night. Let us look up at the moon, the stars and the planets, and watch the majestic Power of the universe at work. We human beings have always found it easy to attribute personality to this mighty Power, whatever our particular persuasion. He is the Creator God whom Christians call Father. Now let us imagine that at this instant we have been transported back into the primeval mists of eternity. What do we find? "God," says my friend Dr. Shadrach Meshach Lockridge, "came from nowhere because there was nowhere for Him to come from. And coming from nowhere, He stood on nothing because there was nowhere for Him to stand. And standing on nothing, He reached out where there was nowhere to reach, caught something when there was nothing to catch, and hung something on nothing, and told it to stay there!"

The Bible is more direct: "In the beginning God created the heavens and the earth." After that we read, "And the Spirit of God was hovering over the waters."[3] Some translators have Him "moving" over the waters, others "brooding," still others (mistakenly, according to the best scholarship) translate "Spirit" as merely "a wind."[4] Franz Delitzsch describes Him as "the creative Spirit of God, the principle of all life."[5]

But why? Why did God create in the first place? Theologians tell us, "For the manifestation of His glory." We look at the night sky in wonder, remember the words of the psalmist: "The heavens declare the glory of God,"[6] and we murmur a word of praise and thanksgiving.

But hold on. Let's become Socratic and pursue our inquiry: Why did God wish to manifest His glory? Was He really aiming it toward us? Are we to understand that the grand object in view of the Creator of the universe was to impress with His Majesty a few of us bipeds who populate a minor planet in a rather insignificant solar system? Does this explanation truly commend itself?

And what about Heaven? The book of Genesis tells us that God created the heaven[s] along with the earth. What is Heaven? The Scriptures don't reveal all we would like to know about it, but they do provide some basic information. Heaven is where God is, and it is a place not only of great glory but also of great joy. Not of pain, or sorrow, or frustration, or boredom, but of joy. If the description given by John in the Book of Revelation is correct—and Christians believe that it is—then Heaven must be a simply marvelous place.[7]

We now have a possible answer to the question, Why did God create the universe? Perhaps He did not create it primarily to demonstrate His power or display His glories. Power impresses and glories dazzle, but joy enthralls. If I read Scripture correctly, God's nature expresses itself most characteristically and distinctively through joy. Thus I dare to suggest that the opening verses of Genesis could mean, "In the beginning, for His own pleasure and joy, God created the heavens and the earth."

The second verse goes on to speak of the Spirit of God "moving" or "hovering over" the waters. But perhaps He was not just hovering; perhaps He was smiling. Perhaps He was rejoicing over the prospect of His new creation. Perhaps again it was an expression of His deepest desire, an outpouring of the sheer, incredible joy which is at the heart of our loving God.

In one of His most significant utterances, Jesus gave this word of cheer to His disciples, "Do not fear, little flock, for it is your Father's good pleasure to give you the kingdom."[8] How much do we know about the Father's good pleasure "which he purposed in himself"? We humans often take pleasure in being creative; why should not God the Creator take joy in what the psalmist calls the work of His fingers? Listen to this word in Isaiah:

> Be glad and rejoice forever
> in what I will create,[9]

and in Zephaniah:

> He will rejoice over you with singing.[10]

That's the word I've been waiting for! When I meditate on the first two verses in Genesis, I think I hear the music of the morning stars. Let us go one better than the airline that claims to fly in "friendly skies." Let us believe God put a song of gladness in outer space; that the mighty galaxies themselves are expressing cosmic joy . . .

> forever singing, as they shine,
> "The hand that made us is divine."[11]

If Addison's poem be true, it's too bad the Soviet cosmonauts didn't catch the music; but they may not have been listening.[12]

Our first premise, based on faith, is that the cosmos we know, the universe that we can view through the giant telescopes, is an expression of joy by the Creator. We establish this premise on the Word of Truth in the Bible, which proclaims that God is love. We can say that God invented the smile if we like, and that He invented human laughter, but we cannot say He invented love because He is love. The mighty machinery of the galaxies is the machinery of His love. The joy that caused the morning stars to sing together was simply the joy implanted by the Creator God Himself acting out of love.

Before we leave the mists of eternity, let us think again about the One who brought into being this magnificent expanse of creation. Theologians have deduced, not from spatial considerations but from their understanding of divine revelation in the Bible, a number of attributes of God which they consider self-evident. These attributes they call divine perfections. The list varies from one theologian to another and one creed to another, but it usually includes the following: God is infinite, eternal, immortal, immutable, illimitable, spiritual, independent, omniscient, omnipotent, omnipresent, sovereign, holy, righteous, wise, good, gracious, merciful, loving, and true.

Did you notice an omission from the list? What about joy? Is not joy an attribute of God? For some reason joy seems to have been downgraded and muted, if not actually overlooked, in theological studies and writings since the days of the apostles. A quick look on any seminary library shelf is sufficient to convince the casual researcher of the absence of joy. Yet surely joy is not incompatible with any of the attributes in the above compendium. If God is perfect holiness, is He not also perfect joy? If He is eternal, is He not eternal joy? My surmise is that at least some members of the scholarly community do not consider joy to be an attribute. Rather they classify it as an emotion more properly associated with human characteristics than attributed to God. In a word, joy in God is an anthropomorphism.

I submit that that is a dubious conclusion and one unsupported by Scripture, which tells us in many ways and places that "the joy of the LORD is your strength."[13]

One final thought as we come back inside from the patio and eternity to time and fresh coffee. Scientists sometimes refer to the material cosmos around us, with all its measurements and facts, as the "given." If we should ask some members of the scientific community whether joy is present in the "given," they would turn toward us with a rather odd look. What? Joy in Arcturus and Betelgeuse? Joy on the moons of Uranus? With palm trees?

The response would be in the negative; we would be informed that the universe is totally insensitive to such emotional qualities. The cosmos is there, it is a datum open to scrutiny as to what it is; but it tells us nothing about origins, where it came from, or why it exists. As for joy, we might look for it among a random assortment of human beings, but nowhere else.

This so-called cosmic silence has one interesting sidelight. Many of the scientists of the past and present who have been exploring the universe believe there is "more out there" than the material facts show. As they see it, the sum of the data, taken together, is greater than the data in the computer. They are convinced that God does in fact reveal Himself in love, that the universe was created in joy and for joy. For one reason or another, many of these scientists are unable to express their faith freely in the classroom, but it is nonetheless genuine. They would agree with the premise of this book, that our Lord Jesus Christ drew His joy from the loving heart of His heavenly Father, the Creator, Maker and Shaper of the universe, who in the fullness of time sent His Son on a mission of redemptive love to the inhabitants of Planet Earth.

Let us by faith examine the record to see whether such benefits are true, and if they are, to see how Jesus went about His mission. Hang on! It should prove interesting.

❁❁❁

➤ *Questions for Discussion*

1. When you think of God, which of these words represent your thinking: joyousness, gladness, delight, pleasure, jubilation? Or do you find these words more accurately reflecting your thought: wrath, gloom, pain, woe, solemnity?

2. The Bible has been branded by many as a "book of doom." Can you suggest reasons it should instead be called a "book of Good News"? What are your reasons?

3. Which way do you picture Jesus—as a driven, sorrowful kind of person, or as a person with a radiant inner happiness? On what do you base your picture? How does it reflect your own outlook on life, and why?

3
Laughter

*How could He be fully man
without laughing at some of the things
that happen in life?
If Jesus wept, He also laughed.*

*I*n the year 1514 a sensational forgery was published in Venice, Italy, purporting to be a description of Jesus Christ by one Publius Lentulus. This Lentulus was said to have been the Roman Procurator of Judea either before or after Pontius Pilate. The Lentulus family was indeed prominent in ancient Rome, and one member actually became Governor of Syria sixty years before Christ. "Publius Lentulus," however, never existed except in the devious mind of some medieval perpetrator of hoaxes.

Nevertheless the forged document has been widely circulated throughout Europe even down to our own time. It was titled "The Epistle of Lentulus to the Roman Senate," and the description of Jesus of Nazareth follows in English translation, as I discovered it in the rare-book room of the Library of Congress:[1]

> "He is a tall man, well shaped and of an amiable and reverend aspect; his hair is of a color that can hardly be matched, falling into graceful curls . . . parted on the crown of his head, running as a stream to the front after the fashion of the Naza-rites; his forehead high, large and imposing; his cheeks without spot or wrinkle, beautiful with a lovely red; his nose and mouth formed with exquisite symmetry; his beard, of a color suitable to his hair, reaching below his chin and parted in the middle like a fork; his eyes bright blue, clear and serene . . . "

In the next paragraph appears the statement that has evidently had a stronger impact on the church than we realize. It seems further to have exercised considerable influence on Christian art over the last several hundred years. The statement reads, "No man has seen him laugh."

The inference is that Jesus never did laugh; that humor, which does so much to alleviate the stress of our daily existence, had no part in His life, and, since we are His followers, it should presumably have no part in ours.

This fraudulent document by the so-called Lentulus, besides being ridiculous, is theologically unsound. Orthodox doctrine since the Council of Chalcedon (A.D. 451) has contended that Jesus Christ is "fully God and fully man."

How could He be fully man without laughing at some of the things that happen in life? If Jesus wept, He also laughed. Laughter is one of the characteristics that distinguish humans from the primates. It is also a characteristic of the Kingdom of God. That, at least, is the way I read the apostle Paul. He wrote to the Romans: "The kingdom of God is . . . joy in the Holy Spirit."[2]

The Bible reminds us again and again of the "voice of mirth." The Book of Proverbs says that the "merry heart has a continual feast"; that such a heart is "good" medicine. The psalmist sings, "Then our mouth was filled with laughter." In another psalm he speaks of "God my exceeding joy." How do we express exceeding joy? What do we do? Isaiah exults, "Sing, O heavens! Be joyful, O earth!" Jeremiah describes the "voice of joy and the voice of gladness . . . of the bridegroom and . . . bride." Jesus told His disciples that after He left them "your grief will turn to joy . . . [which] no one will take away." The apostle Peter confirms that the Christians to whom he is writing "are filled with an inexpressible and glorious joy."[3]

How can we interpret the statement that the seventy evangelists Jesus sent out returned to him "with joy" if we eliminate laughter?[4] What else do we do when we are filled with joy?

In the twelfth chapter of the Letter to the Hebrews is a verse that gives an unusually clear insight into our Lord's mental attitude as He began His ministry. The verse reads: "Let us fix our eyes on Jesus . . . who, for the joy set before him endured the cross, scorning its shame, and sat down at the right hand of the throne of God."[5] Joy? What joy? The joy of Heaven, of course!

Because of Heaven, He could take what He had to face on earth. Because of the thrill and wonder of eternity, He could run the crossfire of time. Because of the glory of God His Father, He could put up with the sinful pride and unbelievable mistakes of the children of men. And because of the presence of the Holy Spirit in Him, He could carry the buoyancy of His eternal joy with Him into the time zone of Palestine, sharing it with others while carrying out His Father's will. "Be of good cheer"—that is, courage! Brighten up! He told His disciples. "There are tribulations in this life, but I have overcome the world."

People have different ways of responding to challenges. Some tighten their belts, spit on their hands, grit their teeth, and throw themselves headlong into it. Some butt their heads randomly against a brick wall. Some laugh helplessly and shrug their shoulders. Some blow their tops indignantly, expressing their anger over the situation—at someone else's expense. Some declare there's nothing to the challenge worth bothering about. Still others sit back and drink the cup of bitterness, predicting failure and virtually ensuring it.

Jesus' way was to face the prospect cheerfully but squarely, without illusions, and to discern through prayer and reflection where His role would be taking Him. He had no tinted glasses. He saw the worst all too clearly, but He also foresaw the great future rewards of His harsh assignments. His work on the cross would bring a Savior to the morally and spiritually desolate human race, and He Himself would leave a clear witness to the love of His Father. After that He would be restored to His rightful place amid the glorious joys and music and laughter of Heaven.

Instinctively we ask whether there is something here for the rest of us. Let's assume I am facing a major problem. I take it to God in prayer, knowing Him to be the real Source of all my joy. Then I turn back to the problem and confront it realistically, in all its ramifications and perils. I estimate what it will take to go through with it, what it will cost in sacrifice and real loss. I consider what good can be

recovered in view of the risk involved, and whether something can someday be done to help others caught in the
same predicament. Then I look beyond the present crisis
to the joy, satisfaction and reward of having done the right
thing in the sight of God, for His sake and also for the sake
of those who love and trust me. This kind of approach has
a noble cast to it; it seems to reflect the mind of Christ; it
also can provide me with a dash of humor as a windbreak
for weathering the storm.

Twin motives set the course of Jesus' life on this earth.
One was the exalted nature of His vocation, which called
Him to save us from our sins and fit us for Heaven. The
other motive was the joyful anticipation of His early return
to His Father. As a consequence He was able to enter upon
His ministry with a blithe touch and a light heart, filled with
the Holy Spirit and with love.

"Don't worry about tomorrow," Jesus advised His
disciples. "Your heavenly Father knows what your needs
are."[6] To Peter's question about John's future prospects,
Jesus replied, "What's it to you? You follow me." And to
the brothers who were quarreling over their inheritance He
said simply, "Who made me a judge over you?" In each
incident you may have noticed a twinkle in the eye or a
disarming smile on the face of our Lord. Perhaps He was
humming a tune or even laughing a little inside. Perhaps
His inner joy was having an effect on His outer behavior.
You didn't catch it? Well—it's a secret! Keep reading.

As Professor John Knox says, Jesus was . . .

> a Man of incomparable moral insight, understand-
> ing and imagination, of singular moral purpose and
> integrity, of extraordinary moral courage and ardor,
> of intense devotion to duty, and [please note] of
> joyous trust in God . . . Although He took life very

seriously, there is no reason to think He took it
solemnly; perhaps He took it too seriously to take
it solemnly . . . [He presented] the whole gamut of
human life with absolute fidelity and with freshness
and great good humor . . . [He] believed that what
is beautiful and good in the world and in human life
is to be enjoyed without apology.[7]

There is a story about an old southern preacher who
was reading from the pulpit out of the seventeenth chapter
of Joshua. He came across the words, "And it came to
pass," and he looked up at his congregation. "Praise the
Lord—isn't He wonderful?" he remarked. "He said it didn't
come to stay; it just came to pass!"

For our Lord, the crucifixion was something to be
undergone. It came, and it passed. The deceased body was
taken down and laid in a tomb, but on Easter morning the
seal on the stone in front of the tomb was broken, and the
risen Jesus came forth in His resurrection body.

Note again: What was His first spoken word? According to Matthew's Gospel, it was addressed to Mary Magda-
lene and the "other Mary" (the mother of James, probably).
They had been to the tomb, had found it empty, had
learned that Jesus had risen, and were running "with fear
and great joy"[8] to tell the disciples about it. Suddenly Jesus
was standing in front of them and speaking. The word He
spoke has been variously translated as "Hail!" "All Hail!"
"Good morning," "Greetings," "Don't be frightened," and
"Peace!"

None of these translations adequately render the
Greek word, which is found in Matthew 28:9. That word
is *chairete*, and it means literally, "Oh joy!" The agony was
finished; the arrest, the trial, the conviction, the sentencing,
the mocking, the beating, the torture, the crucifixion and

the final words all had become part of history. Now the resurrection had taken place as a hard, palpable fact, and everything was changed. As Carl Henry has written, "Without faith that the crucified Christ was alive, the Christian church would never have come into being, nor would we have the New Testament writings."[9] From the risen Jesus' own mouth we hear the word that tells us that the mood of rejoicing had returned: "Oh joy!"

At the close of his book *Orthodoxy*, G. K. Chesterton declares that "joy . . . is the gigantic secret of the Christian." He adds that Jesus, when He came to earth, kept that secret to Himself. "He concealed something . . . He restrained something . . . There was something that He hid from all men . . . some one thing that was too great for God to show us when He walked upon our earth; and I have sometimes fancied that it was His mirth."[10]

There is something about the thought of Jesus' laughter that gives us pause. What was it like? Laughter can be cruel, it can be harsh, derisive, hysterical. A mocking laugh can ruin a career; a savage laugh can lead to murder. Laughter can also be triumphant. Eugene O'Neill wrote a curious drama entitled "Lazarus Laughs," which has one fascinating scene (the rest of the play we can dispense with).[11] In this scene, following the Scriptures, O'Neill has Jesus summon forth Lazarus from his tomb.[12] When the resurrected body of Lazarus dramatically emerges, still wrapped in grave clothes, he (Lazarus) gives a mighty bellow of laughter as if the last enemy, death, had finally been disarmed and vanquished.

If we had been present at those times when Jesus laughed, we might have noticed that His laughter had a similar overtone to it. I can almost hear it, to adapt Tennyson's phrase, echoing down the ringing grooves of time. But in addition to the holy tone of it there was, I believe, something merry about Jesus' laughter that proved infectious. It must have sounded so hearty and warm, so open and appealing! Centuries later the poet Isaac Watts caught the message and unlocked the secret. He wrote that Jesus brought joy to the world and set Heaven and nature singing, so that even the rocks, hills and plains could "repeat the sounding joy."

C. S. Lewis closes his autobiographical book, *Surprised by Joy,* by declaring that joy is really a roadsign pointing us to God; once we have found God, we no longer need to trouble ourselves so much about the quest for joy.[13] I would add that the quest is over. The joy is just "there." It comes with our Lord's prepaid package of salvation, direct from heaven, and furnishes its own proof of authenticity. Richard Rolle, a fourteenth-century English writer, expressed it beautifully: "He who is truly a lover of Jesus Christ does not say his prayers like other men, for seated in his right mind, and ravished with Christ's love above himself, he is taken into a marvelous mirth!"[14]

In 1986 Cal Samra began editing a publication titled "The Joyful Noiseletter" (circulation 10,000) which he sends to a "Fellowship of Merry Christians" from Box 668, Kalamazoo, MI 49005. The rapid growth of this movement and the popularity of Samra's book *The Joyful Christ*[15] suggest that at long last some followers of Jesus are discovering the truth of what Richard Rolle declared so long ago.

As we walk through Galilee with Jesus in the pages that follow, we will be watching for hints of His secret and listening for the sound of His laughter. We will bear in mind both the Source of His joy, and the way He exhibited it, however subtly. But we will not forget that, as important as joy is, it is only one of the attributes of deity, and must never be considered an end in itself. To concentrate on the joy and neglect the Source is to cut off the blossom from the root, to be left with a zephyr, a mere gleam that comes as in a vision, an opiate that quickly vanishes, leaving us yearning and empty. We shall look—and listen—for our matchless, incomparable joy in Jesus, and let the fluttering wings come and go as they will.

❂❂❂

➤*Questions for Discussion*

1. Is it stretching the truth for Rembrandt to paint Jesus as a Dutch burgher, for Korean artists to paint Jesus as an Oriental, for African artists to paint Him black, or for Caucasians to paint Him fair-haired, with blue eyes and a light skin? Does that suggest that Jesus is a construct of the imagination? How would you paint Him?

2. Why do you think artists over the centuries have tended to represent Jesus as a sad or suffering person?

3. In your opinion, what evidence from Scripture can lead you to conclude that on certain occasions Jesus laughed? What difference does this make to you?

4
Religious Smog

"One of the quickest, and on the whole the most effective, ways of getting rid of God is to reverence Him out of existence."
—Dudley Zuver

Years ago while I was serving a student pastorate in northern California, a teenage girl in our church youth group, whose name I have forgotten, asked me a question. She said she was going with a boy of a different faith (a fact I already knew) and certain aspects of church teaching were creating a problem in their relationship. She said she had been to see his pastor who, after he had heard her out, said to her, "My dear, don't you know we're put into this world to suffer?"

I have since found a remarkably similar statement in Thackeray's nineteenth-century English novel, *The Newcomes*. A French priest tries to comfort a long-suffering wife with the words, "Not here, my daughter, is to be your happiness; whom Heaven loves it afflicts."

My teenage friend's question to me was, "Do you think that's right?"

Let me use that girl's question as a springboard to plunge into the real issue, which involves the whole mystery of existence on earth. Her friend's pastor was correct this far: We are born into the world full of suffering, much of which seems to come upon us with no explanation. But does the Bible, the Word of God, really teach that our *purpose* in being born is to suffer? Or is that just some religious smog? To put it into more precise doctrinal terms, does Christianity teach that God is so angry with us over Adam's sin that He has condemned the whole human race to work out its punishment here through suffering? Think a minute. Is that the Good News of the gospel? Is that what Jesus meant when He said, "I have come that they may have life, and have it to the full"?[1]

In Chapter 2, I suggested that Jesus' inner joy came direct from the heart of His heavenly Father by the Holy Spirit, and that probably it was derived also from His mother, who was the daughter of a race known and honored the world over for its cheerfulness, vivacity and ability to laugh even in the most deeply trying circumstances. (Think of the contributions of Jewish comedians.)

Now I would like to suggest a third source of Jesus' joy: the Old Testament.

Let us begin with Psalms, which Jesus seems to have loved and which He often quoted. When I sat down one day and began seriously to look for joy in that book, I became so excited I was (to borrow a phrase my mother often used) "beside myself." I found various forms of the words joy, joyous, enjoy, delight, gladness, and jubilation appearing well over a hundred times, beginning with Psalm 1 and ending with a musical crash in Psalm 150. I am informed that one scholar has listed thirteen Hebrew roots and twenty-seven separate words for joy in the Old Testament writings.[2]

After reading Psalms in my personal devotions for half a century, I was under the common impression that they were rather plaintive in character on the whole, reflecting the hardships and miseries of Palestinian existence. I now realize that nothing could be further from the truth!

The Psalms are above all else hymns of praise and thanksgiving that give a sweet savor and rich perfume to life. They radiate cheer and exhilaration; they sparkle with zest and high spirits. If we have missed that (and for a long time I did), it may be because for centuries we have associated them with a liturgical form that majors on veneration and awe rather than joy. The Psalms are not dirges; they are not wails; overwhelmingly they are the exuberant outpouring of writers who are literally kicking up their heels, so excited are they to discover the redemptive love of Almighty God. "Shout for joy!" "Praise Him with the clash of cymbals." "Praise Him with tambourine and dancing." "Make music to Him." "Praise Him, sun and moon." "Extol the LORD." "My heart leaps for joy." "In your name I will lift up my hands." "The hills are clothed with gladness." "The valleys . . . shout for joy and sing."[3]

Let's continue our quest by researching some other Scriptures. We hear God speaking to the prophet Isaiah in these words: "Shout for joy, O heavens; rejoice, O earth; burst into song, O mountains!" and again, "I will make you . . . the joy of all generations." Nehemiah writes, "The joy of the LORD is your strength." Zephaniah declares, "The

LORD . . . will take great delight in you, he will quiet you with his love, he will rejoice over you with singing." Even the sardonic preacher in Ecclesiastes says plainly, "God gives . . . joy."[4]

Perhaps now you will agree with this position: A case can be made that God's purpose in creation as the Bible sets it forth is inextricably linked to joy. If that be so, then by contrast the history of the church seems to have a hole in it that would match the one in the ozone layer.

Is it possible that the church has been on a two-thousand-year campaign to distill the joy out of Christianity? The Bible tells us that the rivers and trees of the forest clap their hands in praise to God,[5] but in many a church today we are not allowed to clap our own hands. We have turned Isaiah inside out and exchanged the garment of praise for the spirit of heaviness. Joyfulness—exuberance—jubilation—are out of order in our church assemblies. Joy gets scant treatment in our biblical and theological dictionaries. Seldom does it creep into our church histories. It is nowhere to be seen in the records of religious wars, ecclesiastical disputes, persecutions and inquisitions.

Today most worship services in traditional churches are by their nature solemn, although the Psalms themselves are filled with rejoicing. For many people, churchgoing is a matter of duty or obligation; they do not expect to be lifted up. In fact, many come to weep.

Not that Christian joy is altogether ignored in our churches! Eloquent sermons are preached about it and hymns are composed and sung about it, but on the whole the mood in many churches is pretty subdued, if not actually glum. It is taken for granted (what the Bible seems so often to contradict) that solemnity and holiness go together.

Billy Graham states:

> One of the desperate needs among Christian young people is exuberance and vitality in their loyalty to Christ. People go to a football game today and shout their heads off, or go to a circus and cheer act after act. They become enthusiastic about everything conceivable, but when it comes to spiritual matters they think we are supposed to become sober and quiet, and wear black, and never have a good time or enjoy a religious event.[6]

Certainly a frivolous or jocular attitude is inappropriate in approaching the sacred mysteries of our faith, let alone the throne of God Himself. A sense of genuine awe before the Shekinah Glory is indispensable for true worship. The problem with much contemporary worship is not the departure of the divine Presence, for where two or three are gathered together in His name, He still promises to be with us.[7] The problem is the pseudo-spiritual smog we spread over our church life, the unnecessary gravity with which our leadership protects its dignity, the unnatural churchly posturing that so easily passes into overbearing arrogance and conceit.

When I visited C. S. Lewis in Cambridge in 1963 he told me, "There is a great deal of false reverence about. There is too much solemnity and intensity in dealing with sacred matters, too much speaking in holy tones."[8] The tragic loss in all this pious gamesmanship is to the individual in the pew, who begins to feel that in the midst of the religious razzle-dazzle he cannot get through to the Lord Himself.

Dudley Zuver has observed, "One of the quickest, and on the whole the most effective, ways of getting rid of God is to reverence Him out of existence."[9]

Add to the mix the seemingly endless protocol, minutiae and irrelevata that tie our ecclesiastical proceedings in knots, and you have the church of the 1990s, the sacred repository of the most holy faith. To attend many church meetings today is to run the risk of humongous boredom. The "odor of sanctity" turns into polluted air.

Let me go further. Many of the authors of our Christian books seem unable to comprehend what it means to have the kind of radiant, overflowing, inner joy that Jesus brought to earth and shared with His followers. I have known professional theologians who appear baffled and bewildered by a demonstration of the believer's light-hearted joy in the Holy Spirit. To be set free by Jesus Christ, to revel in the new birth, to exude happiness, to celebrate with joy in the knowledge that one's sins have been forgiven because of the vicarious sacrifice of Christ who went to the cross and shed His blood for us and our salvation, is to be—in their words—"an enthusiast." To explain such behavior, they compile erudite monographs about "cultic joy" and "festal joy" and "eschatological joy."

But the joy that today's jubilant new convert has is no different from the joy that Jesus obviously had while He was ministering in Galilee, and which He shared with His disciples. This kind of joy cannot be compartmentalized. It suffuses the whole of existence and blows the dismal clouds of unbelief out to sea. By a miracle of grace the Holy Spirit continues to make it available to us today. It is not mere jolliness, although fun and laughter cannot be ruled out of the Kingdom. What Jesus actually brought with Him from Heaven was something more than a new start for humanity; it was a clear, bubbling, unpolluted delight in God and God's creation, His redemption, His new creation, and His promise of eternal life.

I'm talking about the kind of divine happiness that existed in Paradise before the invasion of evil; or perhaps one was not aware that Adam and Eve were happy? Read the text again. Laughter was born in the Garden of Eden. Elisabeth Elliot reminds us that "obedience always leads finally to joy."[10] Dr. Ed Wheat, a noted marriage counselor, writes:

> As I put the principles of the Bible into practice, and as I learned how really to love my wife, this became pleasure as well as responsibility. Obedience took on the bright colors of joy.[11]

That aptly describes the true situation that existed in Eden at the beginning.

In the chapters that follow we shall be examining the Gospel accounts with a spiritual magnifying glass, searching for clues as to what was going on, how people were feeling, what kind of atmosphere prevailed, and whether there was any joy among the followers of Jesus.

The reason for this research is not simply to add to the massive scholarship that has already been posted in the New Testament field. The true reason for our study is to see whether this New Testament joy can be appropriated today, not just by new converts in the first flush of rapture, but by all of us who love the Lord. Do we have access to it? Is there after all something in Christianity that can make our lives glow, that can turn sorrow into joy, discord into beautiful music, and dreariness into fruitful and abundant living? Did Jesus really bring something from Heaven, something primordial out of the dawn of creation, that can give us the elixir of life which we seem to keep missing?

In his remarkable book, *The Way to Pentecost*, the well-known British Methodist preacher Samuel Chadwick tells us that he was "about my Heavenly Father's business" when . . .

> in my search I came across a prophet, heard a testimony, and set out to seek I knew not what. I knew it was a bigger thing than I had ever known. It came along the line of duty, in a crisis of obedience. When it came I could not explain what had happened, but I was aware of things unspeakable and full of glory.
>
> Some results were immediate. There came into my soul a deep peace, a thrilling joy, and a new sense of power. My mind was quickened. Every power was vitalized. There was a new sense of vitality, a new power of endurance. Things began to happen. It was as when the Lord Jesus stepped into the boat that with all the disciples' rowing had made no progress, and "immediately the ship was at the land." It was gloriously wonderful.

And then he points out that two thousand years ago something very similar happened to those who were present at Pentecost: "Illumination of mind, assurance of heart, intensity of love, fullness of power, exuberance of joy."[12]

> It was a vivid and authentic testimony by an outstanding servant of the Lord. Chadwick then declares that the Holy Spirit is . . .

> the Spirit of Truth, the Spirit of Witness, the Spirit of Conviction, the Spirit of Power, the Spirit of Holiness, the Spirit of Life, the Spirit of Adoption, the Spirit of Help, the Spirit of Liberty, the Spirit of Wisdom, the Spirit of Revelation, the Spirit of Promise, the Spirit of Love, the Spirit of Meekness, the Spirit of Sound Mind, the Spirit of Grace, the Spirit of Glory, and the Spirit of Prophecy.

Great. But not the Spirit of Joy? Why not? Luke tells us that Jesus came into Galilee after His baptism, filled with the Spirit and preaching the Kingdom of God. It was a message of good news and joy. The Book of Acts adds that, during the days after Pentecost, the "disciples were filled with joy and with the Holy Spirit."[13] They were having such a good time people thought they were drunk.

Perhaps you know of a church that is facing a serious crisis. At this moment, while you are reading this page, the church officers are meeting in grave session, trying to cope with a spiritual, moral or financial issue that is threatening to divide the congregation. Other informal groups are meeting privately in homes to express their disaffection. Lengthy telephone calls are being made. Slander is being spread. Petitions are being prepared. Lawsuits are threatened. Members reportedly have been seen attending other churches. As the officers of the congregation meet to grapple with the situation, no one would ever accuse them of being drunk. They are simply earnest Christians trying to make their way through their own religious smog.

Where did we churchfolk lose out? How did we drift so far from the joy of the Lord? Does it not seem strange to you that we should be cut off—amputated—from the hope of the very thing that brought us to church in the first place?

Let's have a look at the Gospels.

❄❄❄

➤ Questions for Discussion

1. What seems to have impressed the citizens of Jerusalem about the behavior of Jesus' disciples at Pentecost?

2. If Christianity was such an experience of joy at its inception, why has church attendance for so many people become a chore?

3. Offer some personal examples to your group of what you consider to be "religious smog." How would you suggest the church attack the problem?

5

Enjoying Him Forever

He was young. He radiated good cheer.
He would have enjoyed taking part
in the banter.

Will you come with me? I am inviting you to a delightful place where there is joy and laughter. We shall climb into our time machine and put the stick into reverse. At some point in the first century we shall disembark in Cana, a village of Galilee, where a wedding is in progress.[1] Jesus and His mother are among the invited guests, and so are the disciples, which of course includes us. That is, some of us. Others of us have been there for some time, doing the serving.

47

It is a lovely occasion and everyone is smiling. Excitement is in the air. The ceremony is being held outdoors in the sunshine. The presence of Jesus lends a touch of glory to the proceedings. Can you imagine anything more thrilling than just being there?

What a pity that so many holy places fail to capture the wonder and joy present at that outdoor wedding. We build churches to honor Jesus, but the net result is usually solemnity, not joy. After a few years the buildings take on a rather gloomy cast. They stand empty so much of the time and are often in disrepair. Many people don't like to enter them. Young Christians seem particularly uncomfortable in them. They prefer to worship in a schoolroom or even a gymnasium, far from the stained glass windows and pulsating organ pipes.

Not long ago Ruth and I visited a European church, a huge pre-Reformation edifice that rose in the middle of a crowded city. Its arches were covered with soot. Underneath in the crypt were the tombs of forgotten saints. The whole atmosphere was on the dreary side. It happened that a noontime weekday service was in progress, and the clergyman was reading Scripture, droning away in the pulpit while three solitary worshipers were huddled in the vast nave. I called to mind what a seminary professor once remarked to our class after returning from an overseas tour. He described the near-empty European cathedrals as "monuments to the memory of God."

Let's go back to our wedding. Why do you suppose Jesus was invited to this event? Was it because He had a face like the shroud of Turin—large, sad, staring eyes and a drooping mouth? I could have told the experts years ago that the shroud was not authentic. People with such faces are not usually seen at weddings. Jesus was no death's head at the feast. Rather He was, if I read the Scripture correctly, a delightful person with a contagious personality—just the kind of individual people like to be around. He exhibited a light spirit. He radiated good cheer. According to the Letter to the Hebrews, He was anointed by His Father with the oil of gladness more than His companions.[2]

That's why Jesus was invited to the wedding. Not because He was a relative they had to invite. Not because He was an apostle of gloom. Not because He was sure to go about buttonholing the other guests and informing them that the fires of hell awaited them. He was invited because He was someone special—a lovable gentle Man and a very warm Friend.

How does this picture compare with other Scriptures that tell us Jesus was a Man of Sorrows and acquainted with grief?[3] Let's note right away that the sorrows and griefs that came later in His ministry were not of His own devising. They played no part in His temperament. Rather they were thrust upon Him from the outside. He was aware that they were coming, He was ready for them, but this wedding took place early in His ministry, and at the moment He was not borrowing trouble or taking thought for the morrow.

Here, then, is the real Jesus, young and fresh, setting out on His heavenly assignment to our planet to bring relief to the hard-pressed human race. What a mission! I recall a popular ballad from my younger days about Casey Jones, a legendary locomotive engineer who, after being assigned to a dangerous run between Lynchburg and Danville, "mounted to the cabin with his orders in his hand."[4] At His baptism Jesus had His orders in His hand. He knew that He was facing a very rough ride, but He was not dismayed or depressed. The New Testament tells us it was because of "the joy that was set before Him [that He] endured the cross, despising the shame."[5]

Our Lord came from Heaven to bring salvation to the world, after which He was going back to Heaven to reign forever. He was sent here to preach the Kingdom of God, to set us free from our sins, and to prepare us for a place in glory. He faced spiritual wickedness in high places, but He was ready to go for it. He was eager and He was happy.

Another trip Ruth and I made recently was to the Philippine Islands. This time we joined a hundred American young people on an evangelistic mission, most of them from a single church. As we waited together in various airports I watched these young men and women gathering in groups, sitting on their packsacks, talking, laughing and singing. They were excitedly anticipating the opportunities stretched out before them, and they seemed completely caught up in the thrill of the occasion. I noticed four young men standing in a group, full of vigor, discussing their street witnessing and spilling over with laughter.

Suddenly it occurred to me that Jesus, about the time He began His ministry, would have fit right into the camaraderie of that group. He was young. He radiated good cheer. He would have enjoyed taking part in the banter. They would have welcomed Him not just with awe and respect, but also with smiles. He would be one with them. Had they been exchanging Scripture verses? He would have one that topped them all. I'm sure a lot of that kind of *koinonia* was going on between Jesus and His disciples in Galilee.

Consider the way He conducted himself with children. As they clustered around Him, probably with their mothers, do you really believe He did not have a smile on His face?

Kids can be cute. They probably felt His beard. Had you showed them a picture of the shroud of Turin, they would have thought it was a Halloween mask. Of course Jesus stopped smiling when His disciples began to interfere with the children, and He had to chide the very men who were so sure they were following Him.[6]

Look at the way He treated women, always with gentleness and respect, always with dignity, in a culture where women were classified with chattel. It was the same with people of other races—the Canaanite woman, the Roman centurion. As for the sick and infirm, He didn't wring His hands over them. He just healed them.

Let's go back again to the wedding. Jesus is stopped by His mother as He walks by her. She tells Him, "They have run out of wine." Many people have difficulty understanding Jesus' reply. I see Him putting His hands on His mother's shoulders and saying with a twinkle in His eye, "Woman, what am I going to do with you? It's not my time!" (When Dostoevsky described this scene in *The Brothers Karamazov,* he added, "He [Jesus] must have smiled gently at her."[7])

Mary may have a premonition of what is coming, for she says to the servants—remember, you and I are among the servants—"Do whatever He tells you."[8] And shortly Jesus orders the six big stone waterpots, that look so much like some of our empty stone churches, to be filled with water. We do it. Then He tells us to draw off some of the water and take it to the host. We do that.

The host tastes what we bring him and his eyebrows go up. He calls the bridegroom over and says to him, "What is going on?"[9] Well, it happens that you and I saw what was going on. We poured the water into those jars. We were aware that Jesus had redirected the processes of nature. We knew; we knew! But the very nature of the miracle was such that in spite of its awesomeness, we were in stitches.

To understand what took place, we have to be in on Jesus' secret. He was a Man of Joy, remember? He was filled with the Holy Spirit and blessed with a light heart. It's hard for us to keep that fact in mind, we are so used to the solemn image and the grim face set "like flint." Since He found Himself at a party, a wedding party, Jesus seems to have decided on a little merrymaking of His own. Customarily at Palestinian festivities the best wine was served to the guests first; later on something akin to rotgut was reserved for those well-blitzed who kept coming back for more. Jesus turned things around, as He often did. He brought in the best at the last—a droll touch, highly amusing and rather startling, but the wedding seems to have lost nothing by it.

Truly to understand this miracle it is necessary to leave the wedding scene and turn to the words of the apostle Paul in Romans 5:5: "The love of God is poured out unto our hearts by the Holy Spirit which is given to us."[10]

At the time of the marriage in Cana the Spirit was not yet given. What Jesus conveyed to the marriage celebrants was a sign which signified the great truth that lay at the heart of His Good News. He was telling them that at just the right time, the water of ordinary conventional religion would be transformed into the wine of a love-filled life by the direct action of God Himself. Jesus' own life would be poured out at the cross for us ungodly sinners, and the water would become wine. The Great I Am would thus enter our orbit from the outside, and by the touch of His Spirit He would light our spirits with His own holy flame, turning our individual lives into vessels of joy and laughter and good news and agape love for everybody. Suddenly we stop all of our pushing and struggling and fighting, and like the Salvation Army lassies, we break out the castanets.

This was to be the gift of Pentecost. This, too, was why Jesus came.

Today, when such an action of the Holy Spirit takes place in an individual life, the ugly spirits of resentment, hostility and bitterness are dissolved by a divine solvent poured into our hearts. Reading the Bible is no longer a chore but a feasting on the Word. Worship becomes a joyous celebration. The casual churchgoer is now a believer, an object of grace and a vessel of love. The water has become wine—not the drug of alcoholic content, but the wine of a contented heart, the wine of peace and gladness.

In a hundred places the Bible tells us that the message of salvation in Christ is a message of joy. The very word *gospel* means "good news, glad tidings." Many of the great hymns of the faith that we sing so solemnly are overflowing with effusions of joy.

What is to keep us from this kind of enjoyment? Must we put a ball to our churches and retrain our song leaders? I don't know. I am no prophet. I have no pill to offer on the market that will produce a sunny disposition and a light heart. But I can tell you how to be filled with the Holy Spirit so that He will give you joy. I've been that route.

The Westminster Catechism declares that the chief end of man (or as we would say, humanity) is to glorify God and enjoy Him forever. I'll let my friends who are better qualified tell you how to glorify Him. My aim in this book is to get you to enjoy Him.

✪✪✪

➢ *Questions for Discussion*

1. What does Jesus' behavior at Cana and Nain tell you about His basic attitude toward life?

2. If you were to decide that, in addition to obeying and serving God, you were going to start enjoying Him, what would you do?

3. What do you think can be done to brighten up places of worship that usually inspire feelings of grayness rather than joy?

6

'Pecooler Noshuns'

*"Your religion is small pertaters, I must say.
You air in a dreary fog all the time."*
—Artemus Ward

Jesus had a sense of humor. It's high time to excavate this truth and examine it objectively. It has been buried too long in the sludge of religious sobriety which is so often mistaken for reverence.

The Gospels abound with evidence pointing to the fact. Jesus' memorable sallies were forever bobbing to the surface in the sacred writings. No wonder His followers found it easy to copy them down! He described the teachers of the Jewish law as "strain[ing] out a gnat and swallow[ing] a camel." He said it was easier for a camel to walk through the eye of a needle

55

than for a rich man to enter the Kingdom of God. He described the care with which the religious leaders washed the outside of their cups before drinking from them but left the inside soiled. He pointed out how ridiculous it was to claim that He was casting out demons by the power of the head demon himself. He advised against casting pearls before swine; He talked about blind men attempting to lead blind men; about dead people burying dead people; about picking figs off a thistle; about hiding a lamp under a bed. He figuratively laughed at people who were quick to point out the speck of dirt in someone else's eye, while they had a plank in their own.[1]

Mention was made earlier about Jesus' attitude toward children. How much good humor was present, do you suppose, as Jesus called the youngsters to Himself and picked up the smallest ones and held them in His lap? Was there intimate talk? Banter? Laughter? Blessing? Did some mother who was present come up with raisin cakes for a treat? What do you think was actually going on when His disciples tried to break up the party?[2]

Or take the famous story of the paralytic whose four friends created their own hospital emergency entrance by tearing open the roof of a house in Capernaum. Their aim was to bypass the crowd around Jesus and get their ailing friend to where he could be helped, so they lowered the mat on which he was lying through the hole in the roof. Jesus "saw their faith," according to the Gospel account, and William Barclay, the Scottish Bible scholar, says, "He must have smiled an understanding smile."[3]

I consider that an understatement. It was a scene hilarious with overtones even though it was not intended to be. Jesus added to the unique mood of the moment by saying the one thing nobody expected him to say: "Son, your sins are forgiven."[4]

The rest of the scene is well known. The paralytic, being human like the rest of us and knowing his own heart, understood what Jesus meant. The theological professionals in the crowd, however, took the remark amiss. Jesus picked up their thoughts and realized they were challenging not the paralytic's need for forgiveness, but rather His own authority. He cleared up that little point by healing the patient. When the crowd (not to speak of the four friends who made up the ambulance) saw the man get up by himself, take his mat, and walk out the door, the roar of excitement and praise that erupted nearly blew off the rest of the roof.

Or take the Syrophoenician woman who knelt at Jesus' feet and implored Him to heal her daughter of an unclean spirit. Jesus looked down at the woman, and again His response was unexpected. He explained that His primary mission was to His own people, and He used a common illustration: "The children's bread shouldn't be given to dogs." Again Barclay suggests that Jesus was "speaking with a smile," and I agree.

This time it seems He probably got a smile back. In making his allusion to children's bread, Jesus had not used the contemporary insulting word for "dog," which is similar to our "bitch." Rather He used the word for "puppy."

The woman looked up at Him and replied in the same light manner, "Yes, Lord, but even the puppies under the table eat the children's crumbs."

What else could Jesus do but laugh? "You win," His attitude implied, and then He told her, "The demon has left your daughter."[5]

If Jesus had a sense of humor, what does that tell us about His Father? Christian faith looks upon Jesus, the risen Christ, as the Second Person of the Holy Trinity, and co-Creator with the Father. "I have never understood," wrote William R. Inge (whom the London press once mocked as the "gloomy dean of St. Paul's"), "why it would be considered derogatory to the Creator to suppose that He has a sense of humor."[6]

More recently D. Elton Trueblood has written, "If Christ laughed a great deal, as the evidence shows, and if He is what He claimed to be, we cannot avoid the logical conclusion that there is laughter and gaiety in the heart of God."[7]

Books have been written about our Lord's wit, His repartee, His keen sense of the absurd, and His ability to see the comical side of a human situation or predicament. Even when no humor whatever is involved, as in the accounts of Jesus' conversations with the woman at the well and the woman "taken in adultery," each dialogue has a unique style, a twist and a flair that betrays the Master's touch.

It is obvious that whatever sense of humor may be ascribed to Jesus was good humor. It derived not from the "swine" of bitterness or cynicism, but rather from the "pearls" of a friendly, good-natured approach to life (the German word is *gemütlichkeit)* which in turn was rooted in a great inner joy, the joy of Heaven.

Thus when our Lord was accused of being what we would call a "wino," He laughed it off. When He was compared unfavorably to John the Baptist, He grasped the opportunity to praise John. And when His disciples were accused of violating the Sabbath by plucking ears of grain,

Jesus took delight in pointing out that David violated the same law at Nob by eating the sacred bread which was reserved for the priests. Not only did David eat it with the sanction of Ahimelech the priest, but he also gave some loaves to his troops, and the whole action had divine approval.[8]

The most significant fact about Jesus that comes through in the Gospel accounts is His happy, radiant, loving personality, so different in character from the solemn religious types He constantly encountered during His ministry. Look, for example, at the way He called His disciples. He visited some fishermen along the shore of the Sea of Galilee and said to them, "Follow me."

It is not clear whether this was their first encounter with Jesus, or whether they had actually met Him earlier or had heard Him proclaiming His message; but the fact remains that they wasted no time in dropping their nets and taking off after Him. In fact, I can hear them saying to one another, "Why not?"[9]

What was the attraction that drew them? Was it His commanding appearance, the impressiveness of His voice of authority, the poor conditions in the fishing industry, the tempting prospectus He set out for them, or some other persuasive factor? What made Levi the tax collector leave his booth and cash box and follow Jesus?[10] Did he think Jesus was a rich man? That He was a dealer in diamonds, or a mysterious stranger with a gold mine in the east? Or that perhaps He was a seer with occultic and magical powers, or even an angel from God?

No. There is only one answer. Jesus was a man of such joy, such merriment, such gladness of Spirit, such freedom and openness, that He was irresistible. They wanted to be near Him, to catch His Spirit, and if possible to learn His secret, to share His joy, and to do what He was doing for other people.

What a pity that Jesus was not presented to succeeding generations as He presented Himself to His own! We are told that great crowds heard him "gladly" and many accepted the good news of the Kingdom that He preached.

Today most pictorial representations of Jesus show Him looking sad, mournful, weeping, in agony of Spirit and body; or else grim and resolute. The very thought of His appearing in a light-hearted or jocular mood is shocking to the religious mind. Even to suggest that He had a warm heart and a fraternal Spirit seems somehow offensive and sacrilegious to many. By some strange twist of interpretation the real Person has not come through in the official annals of the church down through the ages, even though He is palpably present in the Gospel records. The doctrine is there, to be sure. The creeds and catechisms have taken great pains to enshrine the biblical truths, together with all the jots and tittles, but they have not done so well with the Man Christ Jesus.

The rank and file of Christians have done better than the fathers of the church, and have caught something of the Man of Joy and His cheerful message; but so often the religious element predominates, and the joy is lost.

I cannot help believing that Artemus Ward, Abraham Lincoln's favorite humorist, was reflecting the mind of Christ when he told the Pharisees of his day, "Your religion is small pertaters, I must say. You air in a dreary fog all the time, and you treat the jolly sunshine of life as though it were a thief, drivin' it from your doors by them pecooler noshuns of yourn."[11] To which might be added an apposite word from Billy Sunday: "To see some people you would think that the essential of orthodox Christianity is to have a face so long you could eat oatmeal out of the end of a gas pipe."[12]

Earlier in our century neo-orthodox scholars tried to erect a theology that would recover biblical perspectives without invalidating the fruits of modern knowledge. Generally speaking, it could be said that neo-orthodoxy emphasizes the transcendence of God, claiming He is someone "wholly other" than who we think He is. It also emphasizes the sin and guilt of the human race. "The fact that man does evil indicates that he is evil."[13]

The strange result of this theology, which emerged out of the tragedy of the first World War, was that Jesus of Nazareth is exalted as a "mediator" but downgraded as a human being. He is a divine person who invaded the planet to reveal the nature of God as Judge, but it was a "hidden" revelation that was fully disclosed only at His resurrection. Scant attention is paid to the kind of person Jesus was as a citizen of Palestine.

The neo-orthodox theologians declared that the Gospels said virtually nothing about Jesus that today is accepted as authentic. His personality had no real significance then or now. The human predicament was hopeless, they said, and into this situation comes Jesus, the God-man, to heal our "mortal wound." How He does it is not clear—the crucifixion to them remains a mystery—but in some way God bridges the chasm, resolves the contradiction, and makes the reconciliation between God and man. The full revelation of all this occurs in the risen Christ. But instead of the physical miracle of the empty tomb, and the victory over death that was won in the garden of Joseph of

Arimathea, we are left with something nebulous called "Easter faith."

Did Jesus really rise from the dead? When more than five hundred followers saw Him after the crucifixion, did something actually register on the optic nerves of the viewers, or were they merely hallucinating "by faith"?[14] Neo-orthodoxy does not tell us. It refers vaguely to the fifteenth chapter of 1 Corinthians, but it seems more at home in Paul's Letter to the Romans, where it can concentrate on the "human predicament" and its "contradictions."

Many books were published on such themes in the first half of the twentieth century, and they seemed quite similar to biblical truth, particularly on the subject of sin. Some of the old words were used, but with new and apparently different meanings. Eventually someone raised the question, "Where are the songs of neo-orthodoxy?" In other words, where was the joy? The question proved to be a *coup de grâce,* for there were no songs, only a gasp. Neo-orthodoxy had rolled over and expired.

It is tragic that so often in the history of the church, the real Jesus does not come through. The New Testament is a document of great beauty, alive with joy, bright with happiness, filled with love and excitement and healthy teaching for body and soul; yet for millions of people in generation after generation it has remained a gloomy, black-covered book that only tells people how bad they are. So they leave it unopened.

We shall open it.

❁❁❁

➤ *Questions for Discussion*

1. If Jesus truly was a Man of Joy, why is He not shown today as such?

2. If Jesus had a sense of humor, why is this fact not more widely known and better attested to by His followers? Can you suggest ways for the church to use humor more effectively?

3. If Jesus had a merry heart, why has so much Christian music tended to express a somber mood? What can be done about it?

7

Beatitudes

*Love is the first fruit of the Spirit,
and the second fruit is joy. Jesus taught that
for us to feel that love and have that joy, we
must become poor in spirit.*

Blessed are the poor in spirit,
  for theirs is the kingdom of heaven.
Blessed are those who mourn,
  for they will be comforted.
Blessed are the meek,
  for they will inherit the earth.
Blessed are those who hunger and thirst for
      righteousness,
  for they will be filled.
Blessed are the merciful,
  for they will be shown mercy.
Blessed are the pure in heart,
  for they will see God.
Blessed are the peacemakers,

for they will be called sons of God.
Blessed are those who are persecuted because
of righteousness,
for theirs is the kingdom of heaven.[1]

No evaluation of Jesus as a Man of Joy can ignore the Sermon on the Mount. We shall however restrict our attention to the immortal Beatitudes which are recorded in the fifth chapter of Matthew's Gospel, and which appear above.

So many studies have been made and books written about the Beatitudes (I even wrote one myself)[2] that I shall not attempt to add my explanation to all the others as to what Jesus meant when He spoke them. I consider that omission one of the most appealing aspects of this chapter. Anyone with a grain of common sense should know what Jesus meant by the terms, "the merciful," "the peacemakers" and "the pure in heart." Why should I "explain" them?

It amuses me to recall what one Bible commentator wrote about the "first love" that Jesus mentions in His letter to the Ephesians as found in Revelation 2:4. This erudite scholastic said, "The 'first love' of the Ephesians was the love which they had at the first." That about does it for the Beatitudes too. Perhaps I can explain that when Jesus said, "Blessed are the meek," He was referring to people who are meek. End of Bible lesson.

If my remarks seem facetious, I am only protesting against the insufferable heaviness of so much biblical scholarship. Here is a superb message of joy leaping out of the past, a gorgeous and dazzling epic of vivacity, color and pristine truth, and the pedants treat it as if it were the driest subject imaginable. I would as soon try to computerize the number of molecules in a rainbow. But in order to avoid the treacherous bog of criticism, let us turn instead to one word in the Beatitudes that is completely fascinating.

We shall look at the first word Jesus spoke in his Sermon on the Mount, *Blessed.* In the original Greek manuscripts the adjective is *makarios,* which is not easy to render into ordinary American usage. To begin with, the word *blessed* itself is not an expression we use every day in our shopping malls. Yet when the effort is made to find some other word than *blessed* to translate *makarios,* something of the meaning is lost. Many translators have substituted the word *happy* for blessed; but happy, like *hapless,* is derived from the Old Norse root *happ* which means simply luck or chance. Thus when a person wins a lottery or otherwise "gets a break," we consider he or she is happy. That has nothing to do with blessedness. For the Christian no accurate synonym exists for the hallowed words *bless* and *blessing.*

I like what Dr. William Barclay has to say:

> The blessedness which belongs to the Christian is not a blessedness which is postponed to some future world of glory; it is a blessedness which exists here and now. It is not something into which the Christian will enter; it is something into which he has entered. It is a present reality to be enjoyed. The Beatitudes in effect say, "O the bliss of being a Christian! O the joy of following Christ! O the sheer happiness of knowing Jesus Christ as Master, Savior and Lord!" The very form of the Beatitudes is the statement of the joyous thrill and the radiant gladness of the Christian life. In face of the Beatitudes a gloom-encompassed Christianity is unthinkable.
>
> *Makarios* then describes that joy which has its secret within itself, that joy which is serene and

untouchable and self-contained, that joy which is completely independent of all the chances and changes of life. The Beatitudes speak of that joy which seeks us through our pain, that joy which sorrow and loss, pain and grief are powerless to touch, that joy which shines through tears, and which nothing in life or death can take away.

The world can win its joys and the world can equally well lose its joys. But the Christian has the joy which comes from walking forever in the company and in the presence of Jesus Christ. The Beatitudes are triumphant shouts of bliss for a permanent joy that nothing in the world can ever take away.[3]

In ancient Greece *makarios* was a poetic word that referred to the blessedness of the gods. According to Kittel, the Hebrew word for blessed signified fullness of life.[4] True blessedness in the Old Testament consisted of trust in God, forgiveness of sins, righteousness even in affliction, and final deliverance. The New Testament on the other hand uses *makarios* as a term for the distinctive joy which comes through participation in the divine kingdom.

I see five unique characteristics of the word *blessed* as Jesus used it in the Beatitudes:

1. Something is bestowed or given. Jesus does not imply in any of the Beatitudes that we earn anything by our own spiritual efforts. If however we exhibit certain qualities, blessing comes.

2. God is the one who bestows the blessing. Almost always in Scripture when the word blessing is used, it has some kind of reference to God. He gives the blessing. Happiness on the contrary is not usually associated with a divine origin.

3. The blessing is a big one. The Greek word *maka-rios* comes from the root *mak* which is also the root of *macro,* a common English prefix to signify something large. Jesus implies that when God sends a blessing He makes it big!

4. The blessing lasts. The same Greek root that means large can also mean lengthy. A blessing from God has an enduring quality, as Mary realized during her visit to Elizabeth.[5]

5. The blessing is always good. The merchandise of God is sheer goodness. The teachings contained in the Beatitudes are still the highest principles of human behavior, and are recognized as such all around the world. They remain the only basis for civilized living.

To sum up, the blessings Jesus spelled out in the Beatitudes are unmerited gifts, they are bestowed upon us by God, they are immense, they last, and they are chock full of goodness.

Note one other thing: In most of the Beatitudes Jesus used the future tense. The words *shall* and *shall be* occur several times. Thus the blessed joy that comes to the mourner is not his mourning; it is the comfort that will come afterward. Jesus always seems to be looking to the bliss that lies ahead, and Jude reminds us that we should be too, for one day we will be presented "before his glorious presence without fault and with great joy."[6] With Jesus, anticipation never exceeds realization.

And finally I would speak of one Beatitude that has been the subject of considerable confusion. It is the first one: "Blessed are the poor in spirit, for theirs is the kingdom of heaven."[7] Luke, in his version of this Beatitude, omits "in spirit," leaving us with "Blessed are you poor, for yours is the kingdom of God."[8] This difference in wording has led some Bible students to suggest that the phrase "in spirit" was not actually spoken by Jesus but was added, as they like to say, "by a later hand." Presumably the hand belonged to some ecclesiastically minded functionary in the early church who had some theological point he wanted to make. The whole theory is based on the supposition that Jesus was deeply involved in the problem of poverty, which He saw as the cause of all social ills.

I do not intend to play off Luke's Beatitude against Matthew's. I do wish to defend Matthew's version as authentic, because in it Jesus lays the foundation of all His teaching about the Holy Spirit.

The reason so many earnest, sincere believers are failing to find joy in their Christian life is that they are not filled with the Spirit. And the reason they are not filled with the Holy Spirit is that they are occupied with all the unholy spirits—that is to say, the negative attitudes—and these spirits monopolize the believers' time and effort: hostility, resentment, fear, bitterness, envy, revenge, antagonism, arrogance, self-love . . . the list goes on and on. How can one enjoy the fullness of the Holy Spirit, who is God, when one is filled with everything else?

To be filled with the Spirit is to be filled with love. Love is the first fruit of the Spirit, and the second fruit is joy.[9] Jesus taught that for us to feel that love and have that joy, we must become poor in spirit.

That does not mean to become a wisp or a wimp. Meek has never meant weak. Someone has defined meekness as power under control. To be poor in spirit means that we have shucked off the zeal so often compounded with corruptible human pride. We may not see it in ourselves but other people do. They see us strutting like turkey cocks. Get rid of it, Jesus is saying. Grow up. Become a full-grown person, mature, operational.[10] As Irenaeus said in the second century, the glory of God is a man fully alive.[11] He could have said the same thing about a woman—and added an exclamation point! But to be alive is to be alive in God, to be God-controlled, not to be a pious nothing with a hand-crafted halo and a reputation for being "religious."

When I hear people talk on the subject of "spiritual growth" I send up a red flag. I can't help it. I know there is such a thing as spiritual growth, and I salute it and believe in it. But in my own life I have learned that a lot of such growth consists simply of my getting out of God's way. It is actually shrinkage rather than growth. I am certain that God does not want me to develop into a spiritual giant in my own eyes, even if I could. He wants me to become a spiritual pygmy so He can handle me. He wants me poor in spirit so He can do something with me without His having to contend with my ever-present, darling ego.

Jesus told about a man who prayed, "God be merciful to me a sinner!"[12] That man, he said, went down to his house justified. He had built his house upon a rock: God's mercy to him in the midst of his sin. That's what it means to be poor in spirit.

It is when we let go of the rope that we discover that underneath are the everlasting arms. It is when we have no spirit at all, as far as the "flesh" is concerned, that we are able to receive the filling of the Holy Spirit. That is the work of the cross in Christian experience. As Paul wrote, "We have this treasure in earthen vessels, that the excellence of the power may be of God and not of us."[13]

Oh, the joy that comes when people realize they don't have to be religious with God, they don't have to be sanctimonious, they don't have to be anything or do anything except repent and believe the Good News! All the blessing of the Father, the love of Jesus, and the joy of the Holy Spirit are theirs for the taking. Of such indeed is the Kingdom of Heaven.

☺☺☺

➤*Questions for Discussion*

1. How are happiness and blessedness similar? How are they different?

2. What would you consider to be some of the evidences of true spiritual growth? Use your own spiritual condition as an illustration.

3. How does being what Jesus called "poor in spirit" characterize a fruitful Christian life?

8

The Ultimate

*If they could win the lottery, or
if someone would just die and leave them
some money, then Mudville would become
Joyville. But as it is . . .*

After listening to Beethoven's Fifth Symphony, Paul Claudel, the French poet, is said to have remarked, "Now I know that at the heart of the universe there is joy."[1] Earlier chapters asked where joy came from, and now we know. We have verification that it came from God Himself. It was there at the beginning (there was a beginning!) when the Creator purposed to bring creation into existence. By His will, joy became part of the moral grain of the universe.

We have learned that joy is more than a sense of the comic, more than earthly pleasure, and to a believer more even than what we call happiness. Joy is the enjoyment of God and the good things that come from the hand of God. If our new freedom in Christ is a piece of angelfood cake, joy is the frosting. If the Bible gives us the wonderful words of life, joy supplies the music. If the way to Heaven turns out to be an arduous steep climb, joy sets up the chair lift.

The fact is, joy is an attribute of God Himself. It has the authentic stamp of the *ultimate*. It brings with it pleasure, gladness and delight. Joy is merriment without frivolity, hilarity without raucousness, and mirth without cruelty. Joy is sportive without being rakish and festive without being tasteless. Joy radiates animation, sparkle and buoyancy. It is more than fun, yet it has fun. It expresses itself in laughter and elation, yet it draws from a deep spring that keeps flowing long after the laughter has died and the tears have come. Even while it joins those who mourn, it remains cheerful in a world that has gone gray with grief and worry.

Joy is not a mere sentimental word. It has a clean tang and bite to it, the exhilaration of mountain air. That's because it blows away the dustiness of our days with a fresh breeze, and makes life more carefree. Perhaps the French translators of the Bible were attempting to say something like that when they rendered the third Beatitude, "Blessed are the debonair, for they shall inherit the earth."[2] The French apparently see a carefree quality in meekness and humility that most of us miss. And is joy carefree? Is joy "debonair," that is, light-hearted, genial and gracious? You decide.

For many, pleasure and happiness are but fleeting experiences in life. Goethe at the age of seventy-five admitted that he had known only four weeks of happiness. There are Christians, some of them victims of lifelong suffering, who could say the same thing. But joy! Here we move into a different dimension, and that telltale light comes into the eye of the believer. Joy is not happiness so much as gladness; it is the joy of salvation, the exultation of God's Spirit in men and women, "good measure, pressed down, shaken together and running over."[3]

Joy was set before Jesus while He was on earth; it was a joy both present and in prospect. For today's Christian, fulfillment is never quite complete but there is always joy in prospect. Thus joy becomes the ecstasy of eternity in a soul that has made peace with God and is ready to do His will, here and hereafter.

To think of joy in mundane terms as something that accompanies victory in a contest, or the accomplishment of some difficult task, may seem legitimate, but it obscures the full, rich meaning of the word. Today we may be jubilant over our team winning a game; tomorrow we have the blues because our team lost. The ending of Ernest Lawrence Thayer's famous rhyme, "Casey at the Bat," says it well:

> Oh, somewhere in this favored land
>   the sun is shining bright;
> The band is playing somewhere,
>   and somewhere hearts are light;
> And somewhere men are laughing,
>   and somewhere children shout,
> But there is no joy in Mudville—
>   Mighty Casey has struck out.[4]

And that is just where so many Christians are today— in Mudville. They thought that if Casey slammed the ball out of the park, life would be ice cream and chocolate mousse. If they could win the lottery, or if someone would just die and leave them some money, then Mudville would become Joyville. But as it is . . .

To pin one's hopes solely on such earthly events is in a sense to couple joy to a slot machine that has been fixed. Human history virtually guarantees that we, like Casey, will strike out. Our exuberance at any given moment vanishes into thin air. That is the curse that sin has laid upon our planet. We need to find something less ephemeral and fleeting than Casey's bat, something that will keep the joybells ringing even when there is nothing to celebrate.

That "something" can be found in the pages of the New Testament. It tells us that our biggest problem on earth—how to face a holy God just as we are—has already been solved. We can relax. The sacrifice has been made, the Lamb of God has been slain, the price has been paid, the blood has been shed for our redemption. Our sins are forgiven, and our future is secure. Thanks to the saving grace of our Lord Jesus Christ, the ticket to Heaven is already in our pocket.

Trueblood wrote in 1964:

> The Christian is [joyful], not because he is blind to injustice and suffering, but because he is con-vinced that these, in the light of the divine sover-eignty, are never *ultimate*. The Christian can be sad, and often is perplexed, but he is never really worried, because he knows that the purpose of God is to bring all things in heaven and on earth together under one head, even Christ.[5]

Some time back I attended a Christian concert by black musicians, in which four young men sang a quartet number which told more about the *ultimate,* more about the excitement and joy of Heaven, than I ever could. It went like this:

"Sit down, brother."
"Can't sit down."
"Sit down, brother."
"Can't sit down."
"Sit down, brother."
"Can't sit down. I just got to Heaven and I
can't sit down!"

Now let me assume that it is evening, and while you read this you are watching the six o'clock news telecast. Too often it is the grimmest hour of the day. You are bombarded with an appalling succession of visual images that reveal the human race in the throes of mortal agony. Nearly every sound bite depicts angry demonstrators, corpses being carried out, or people existing in dire need—need that is not being met, cannot now be met, and may never be met.

Is this all there is to life? And is Christianity an equally dismal and depressing trip, a sorrowful and woebegone Via Dolorosa? Is our existence on this planet a cosmic tragedy, and is the Bible a kind of moralistic stepmother, a Miss Manners directing us to quit whatever it is we are doing and do something else?

I object. This is a caricature of Gospel truth. No one can mourn or weep for long when Jesus is around. Depressed spirits simply cannot stay depressed in His presence. Scripture itself tells us that on the evening of the day when He rose from the dead, Jesus came into the room where the disciples were gathered and stood among them. What was the reaction? "The disciples were overjoyed when they saw the Lord."[6]

No matter how bad the bad news is (and as Aldous Huxley once wrote, the news is always bad), the Gospel of our Lord Jesus Christ is, by contrast, glad tidings of great joy. God loves us. He wants us to leave our sinful ways and forsake our grousing about life. He wants us to get on top of life, to stay out of the dumps, and to encourage others to do the same. He wants us to be filled with the Holy Spirit and with joy.

In the Book of Acts is a story about the apostle Peter, who was miraculously delivered from the prison of King Herod Antipas by an angel. According to Luke, who tells the story, Peter found himself walking on a street in Jerusalem in the middle of the night. He proceeded to a "safe house," the home of John Mark's mother, and knocked at the door.

A girl named Rhoda answered the knock, opened the door, and recognized Peter. She was so astonished at seeing him that she forgot to invite him in. Instead she left him standing outside, shut the door, and ran inside to break the news.

An all-night prayer meeting was in progress, and people were on their knees interceding on Peter's behalf. When Rhoda interrupted them, nobody believed her, because they all knew that Herod had arrested Peter and had set the execution for the next day.

Peter meanwhile remained outside, continuing to knock. Finally someone went to the door, opened it and let him in, whereupon, in Luke's chaste language, "they were astonished."[7]

That story is a parable of the way Christians often live. We discover the truth of the Gospel; we recognize it; we acknowledge it; we believe it; we are so impressed with it that we even go and tell others about it; we are persuasive; but we forget the one thing that speaks louder than all our words. We leave the joy standing outside. We draw the bath but ignore the baby. People look at us, listen to us, and gradually tune us out. They decide Christianity is just one more option, one more thing, and what difference does it make anyway?

Professor Gordon Allport, the distinguished American psychologist, gives us a different picture of the role of the *ultimate* in preserving joy in the heart of a believer:

> What keeps the religious person from becoming a cynic—as all thoroughgoing humorists must be— is the conviction that at bottom something is more important than laughter, namely, the fact that he, the laugher, as well as the laughter itself, has a place in the scheme of things according to the dispensations of a Divine Intelligence. When this most important of issues is decided, there is still plenty of room for jesting.
>
> In fact, a case might be made for the potentially superior humor of the religious person who has settled once and for all what things are of ultimate value, sacred and untouchable, for then nothing else in the world need be taken seriously. He can readily concede that the bulk of worldly happenings are ludicrous, that men and women, including himself, are given to amusing vanities, actors on a stage set with human artifices.
>
> To him nothing in their coming and going is of consequence, except their *ultimate* salvation. Most things they do are merely laughable. Beyond the reach of humor lies one and only one serious purpose to which humor must give way whenever the two are in conflict. Plenty of amusing episodes occur in church. It is only the *ultimate* aim of the acts of worship that, for the religious person, lies beyond the scope of humor."[8]

So now we know what joy is, and what it is built upon: the *Ultimate.* We know what it does, and we have been told where to look for it: in the New Testament. What does the New Testament say?

It says:

The kingdom of God is not a matter of eating and drinking, but of righteousness, peace and joy in the Holy Spirit . . .

May the God of hope fill you with all joy and peace as you trust in him . . .

The fruit of the Spirit is love, joy, peace . . .

If you obey my commands, you will remain in my love . . . I have told you this so that my joy may be in you and that your joy may be complete . . .

We write this [to you] to make our joy complete.[9]

Are you beginning to catch on? Joy comes by way of the Holy Spirit! He is God; God is love; and love, when it has free course, always expresses itself in a joy whose roots lie in the *Ultimate.*

❈❈❈

➤ *Questions for Discussion*

1. When Nehemiah writes that "the joy of the LORD is your strength," is he referring to our joy in the Lord, or the Lord's joy in us, or both? Give reasons for your personal view.

2. How are the words *joy* and *happiness* alike? How are they different?

3. In Christian terms, is it more accurate to say that joy is an expression of love, or that love is an expression of joy? On what do you base your conclusion? Can you illustrate your view from your own life?

9

Celebrate!

If I have faltered more or less
In my great task of happiness . . .
Lord, thy most pointed pleasure take
And stab my spirit broad awake.
                    —Robert Louis Stevenson[1]

*I*t's a curious thing. Whenever I bring up the subject of "joy" in conversation, people's faces seem to light up, but when I switch to the word "rejoice," the luster begins to fade. Why?

The dictionary tells me that "rejoice" is an intransitive verb that requires no object. It means to be glad, to enjoy, to take delight in something, to be thankful, even to "feel good." Yet for some reason the word is no longer in common American usage; evidently it has lost some of its popularity. The present generation is not well acquainted with it. The business and advertising community, I believe, considers it archaic.

The one scene where "rejoice" seems to fit is in church. It is a staple item in the religious jargon. Many Christians regard it as a perfectly good, rather formal word and use it a great deal. Hardly a Sunday passes in the average church without a clergyman "rejoicing" about something. We read it in the hymnals and in church newsletters. If there is good news to impart, there is "cause for rejoicing."

However, just how people go about doing it is not clear. I do remember being told of an elderly lady testifying that she had only two teeth left in her mouth, and she was "rejoicing" because "they hit."

The counsel that Christians find in the Gospels and letters of the New Testament is to rejoice and keep on rejoicing. Whatever the word means, surely it does not mean to become like the well-known Canadian river— frozen at the mouth.

Here are some choice New Testament selections:

[Jesus said], Do not rejoice that the spirits submit to you, but rejoice that your names are written in Heaven . . .

I will see you again and you will rejoice, and no one will take away your joy . . .

[Paul said], We rejoice in the hope of the glory of God . . .

In every way Christ is preached . . . I rejoice . . . and will continue to rejoice . . .

My brothers, rejoice in the Lord! . . .

Rejoice in the Lord always. I will say it again: Rejoice! . . .

The whole crowd of disciples began joyfully to praise
God in loud voices for all the miracles they had
seen.[2]

And here are some Old Testament passages on the
same theme:

You shall rejoice in all the good things the LORD your
God has given to you and your household . . .

Let the hearts of those who seek the LORD
rejoice . . .

May the righteous be glad and rejoice before God;
    may they be happy and joyful . . .

Will you not revive us again, that your people may
rejoice in you? . . .

Blessed are those who have learned to acclaim you,
who walk in the light of your presence, O LORD.
They rejoice in your name all day long; they exult in
your righteousness . . .

Let the heavens rejoice, let the earth be glad;
    let the sea resound, and all that is in it;
    let the fields be jubilant, and everything in them.
Then all the trees of the forest will sing for joy . . .

Shout for joy, all the earth,
    burst into jubilant song with music . . .

He brought out his people with rejoicing,
    his chosen ones with shouts of joy . . .

I rejoice in your statutes . . .

May you rejoice in the wife of your youth . . .

When the righteous thrive, the people rejoice . . .

When the righteous triumph, there is great
    elation . . .

The humble will rejoice in the LORD . . .

> I will rejoice in doing them good . . . The LORD your
> God is with you,
>   He is mighty to save.
> He will take great delight in you,
>   he will quiet you with his love,
>   he will rejoice over you with singing.[3]

What an effusion of divine joy and exultation! It seems
to set the whole universe to music, and to create a chorus
among the very creatures of the earth. It carries a triumphant note, a note of high spirits, ecstasy, elation, transport
and rapture. No drug trip was ever like this. No humanly
induced state can compare with it.

But wait a minute. What does it mean, really, to
rejoice? Does it create a difference in our outward behavior? Does it motivate us to do something? When we are
rejoicing, do we treat people in a special way? Once I asked
a Christian brother, "How are you?" and he replied,
"Rejoicing." It brought me up short. Rejoicing about what?
I wondered. He didn't say, nor did he ask me how I was.
Our conversation (if you call it that) rather petered out.

Let's look further into that word *rejoice*. It is still an
intransitive verb; it doesn't tell us what to do, or even
whether to do anything at all. Thus it is not fully capable
of conveying the message of joy that God is obviously
seeking to impart. I have gone over all the synonyms: revel,
be glad, enjoy, and many others. They are great words,
and they all have a more contemporary sound than "rejoice," but I have come to appreciate one other word that
seems to ring the bell even louder in speaking to our
generation.

That word is *celebrate*. It is a transitive verb. It renders
with reasonable accuracy the Hebrew and Greek originals.

It requires an object. Let's see what it does for the Old Testament if we substitute it for *rejoice*:

> Let the hearts of those who seek the LORD celebrate . . . Let the heavens celebrate, and let the earth be glad . . . When the righteous thrive, the people celebrate . . . The LORD your God will celebrate over you with singing.

And now the New Testament:

> I will see you again and you will celebrate, and no one will take away your joy . . . We celebrate in hope of the glory of God . . . My brothers, celebrate in the Lord! . . . I will say it again: Celebrate!

But again, wait: what about the object? Celebrate how? Celebrate what? It is not a question of "feeling good"; we have here a summons to action, whether to celebrate a birthday, or an anniversary, or a patriotic holiday, or even the Lord's Supper! Today the word "celebration" is more popular than ever with people everywhere.

Some of us who have spent years in evangelistic activity are noticing a change in this direction. Younger evangelists are moving into a mood of celebration and a more festival-oriented type of outreach, particularly in third world countries. With drama groups, musicians, special teams of carpenters, medical personnel, and athletes; with ministries targeted to the homeless, the undernourished, the sick, the incarcerated, and the needy; with street evangelists, mimes, well-known local personalities, parades, balloons and fireworks, young men and women are carrying the message of Christ into the great population centers of several continents. They are doing so with a fervor and a wave of excitement that is reminiscent of the early days of the Jesus Movement.

This ministry is in its early stages, but it seems to be riding the wave of the future. Its atmosphere of celebration is proving to be a powerful attraction as the public at large grasps the idea that Christianity is in the business not of taking but of giving, not of dispensing gloom but of spreading good cheer.

The injection of a spirit of jubilation is in no way diluting the force of the saving gospel message any more than it did two thousand years ago in Galilee. Typically, after a period of worship and praise in such meetings, the message of salvation is preached to the gathering. But the message is not "Sinners in the Hands of an Angry God."[4] It is a message of grace and deliverance from sin by the death and resurrection of Jesus Christ, a call to repentance, commitment and new life in the Spirit. It is a life not only victorious, but filled with the joy of Heaven. Gone are the somber trappings and overtones of doom. It is the grand old Gospel singing a new song, arrayed in a twenty-first-century format, drinking at the old fountain that never runs dry.

The church has been given a joyful message. It is the greatest news that ever came to the human race. No religion in the world can come up with anything to match the Gospel in its assurance of God's love and His promise of salvation. But so often it happens that the church has all this rich golden ore and doesn't know how to refine it, so it transmutes the feelings of joy into feelings of reverence, not realizing that in Scripture the two go together.

We are taught since childhood what to do when trouble comes: "Take it to the Lord in prayer." We cast our cares on Him because He cares for us. We cast our cares, but not our joy, if you please. The joy we keep, for joy is a gift from God and shouldn't be transmuted into anything.

Instead of subduing our joy and leaving it outside in the church parking lot, we should be expressing it and making it the accompaniment of everything we do, both in and out of church, just as the Creator Himself infused joy into His whole vast mechanism of creation.

Veneration and respect are always due to our blessed heavenly Father. We are commanded to worship Him in the beauty of holiness, but for Heaven's sake let's not lose the joy in the midst of it. Let's not worship by transposing our thoughts into an everlasting minor key. God's word to Isaiah is: "I will . . . give them joy in my house of prayer."[5] Let's find it! The Psalms tell us to make a joyful noise to the Lord, to praise Him with all manner of instruments and our own shouts of gladness; and yet—there is a time for keeping silence before Him. That too is scriptural and has a high priority, for how can God communicate to us during our prayers if we keep up a continual patter rehearsing all our unmet needs? Too many words can drown out the Word—which leads me to another thought.

I used to wonder why Jesus, after His resurrection from the grave, chose to go back to Galilee.[6] His disciples and other followers had come from there, and it was only natural for them to set their faces toward home after the terrible events in Jerusalem. But why Jesus? He had made it clear that He was returning to Heaven to be with His Father. Why the side trip to Galilee? Obviously He had arranged the reunion because He had some extremely important things to say to His disciples once they got there.

It has occurred to me that Jesus went back to Galilee for another reason. It was because that was where He had such rich memories of joy. Galilee was where His Father had spoken to Him, where His ministry had been so marvelously blessed and had brought such joy to people, where He had walked among the lilies in the fields, had climbed the hills, and had sailed upon the lake. Galilee was where He had gathered His friends and began His church. It was where He prayed alone, and kept silence.

Have you never yourself returned to some spot on this earth where your memories are still bright and beautiful? Where you looked upon scenes that reminded you of past events, when you were younger, perhaps, and full of the excitement of living and tingling with hope?

I could be wrong, but I think Galilee was very special to our Lord. This time when He returned He again roamed the hills and walked along the lakeshore. It's true He had a ministry to complete, but there may have been an added incentive. The agonizing struggle was ended, the sacrifice was complete, and His mission on earth was about to close. Perhaps He wanted to look once more on the scenes He loved so well—and to celebrate by cooking breakfast for his friends.[7]

❁❁❁

➤ *Questions for Discussion*

1. What, if any, significance do you attach to Jesus' return to Galilee following His resurrection?

2. How would you say the words *rejoice* and *celebrate* are alike and how are they different, particularly in terms of action?

3. Can you distinguish a difference between the terms reverence and solemnity? Apply them to your own feelings about worship. Which is appropriate, for example, at a wedding? Or at a funeral? Why?

10

Parables

They were celebrating because
He was with them.
What's wrong with having some joy in life?

Nearly everybody likes to tell stories, and few things that we do betray our true nature more openly than the kind of stories we tell. When a person becomes a Christian, his friends listen—perhaps unconsciously—for signs of change in his story-telling. Has the Holy Spirit really worked on him? To adopt a new vocabulary is easy; to change one's stories is a matter of a different order.

A characteristic of Jesus Christ that has fascinated men and women for centuries was His tendency to tell interesting stories. The fact that He deliberately used fiction instead of polemic has often been cited as a key to His popularity over the centuries. Whenever Jesus began with "The Kingdom of Heaven is like . . . " people seemed to find His words irresistible, and they still do. He did not tell jokes or spin yarns or make up tall tales. Sometimes He used a wry humor, sometimes not; but always His stories were vivid, and they tell us a lot about Him—His nature, what He was really like. The Gospel writers called His illustrations parables.[1]

According to Kittel, a parable technically is more than a simile or a metaphor; it is "a similitude which uses evident truth from a known field (nature or human life) to convey new truth in an unknown field (the kingdom of God)."[2]

We are given to understand that the parables were typical of our Lord's method of instruction. We shall therefore look at a few of them closely to see whether they yield any clues to the subject of our investigation.

Instinctively I turn to the fifteenth chapter of Luke, in which are recorded the parables of the lost sheep, the lost coin and the lost son.[3] It is not surprising that we are now in one of the most popular chapters of the New Testament. Here are three stories, each with a joyful ending. Let us see if they reflect Jesus' secret.

The first thing to note is the setting. After dining at the home of a Pharisee, Jesus emerges and finds a large gathering of "sinners and tax-gatherers" who have come to hear Him, much to the displeasure of certain religious leaders including, perhaps, his host. Jesus then tells the parable of the lost sheep.

The owner of a hundred sheep learns one is missing, goes after it, finds it, lays it on his shoulders, and comes back exulting with joy. He calls together his friends and neighbors and says, "Come and celebrate with me; I have found my sheep that was lost."

Jesus then added that there is more celebrating in Heaven over a repentant sinner than over ninety-nine "righteous ones who need no repentance."

Next, the parable of the lost coin is presented in the form of a question. If a woman has ten silver coins (drachmas) and finds one of them is missing, does she not light a lamp and sweep the house until she finds it? And having found it, does she not call in her friends and neighbors and say to them, "Celebrate together with me, for I have found the coin I lost"?

After relating the parable, Jesus added that when the angels of God hear of one sinner who has repented, they burst out with joy.

The parable of the lost son, which follows the first two, gives us a lengthier opportunity to study our subject. Remember, we are not engaged in a full-dress exegesis of the passage. We are only looking for clues to the temperament, demeanor and disposition of Jesus as He went about His ministry. We know He did not approve of the "downcast faces" of the "hypocrites" who wanted people to know they were engaged in pious fasting. Fasting for God is good, but be cheerful when you do it; wash your face and anoint your head, and act as if you aren't fasting. As for your prayers, avoid ostentation. Don't cultivate salutations in the marketplaces, or maneuver for the best seats at feasts or in the synagogue.

But what did Jesus say that discloses what He was actually like? In this parable we find Him describing a father of whom He thoroughly approves. Some Bible scholars contend that the father in the parable should not be identified with the heavenly Father. We will not debate that issue, but will simply say that Jesus obviously considered this particular father's behavior to be exemplary.

The younger of the man's two sons asks for his share of the property and the father arranges to give it to him. The young man takes it, travels to a distant land, and wastes his bequest in dissolute living. Penniless in a famine-ridden land, he hires himself to a pig farmer, and finds himself so hungry he wants to eat the husks he is feeding to the pigs. He "comes to himself," decides that his father's farmhands are eating better than he, and goes home ready to confess his unworthiness and to repent of his sin.

To this point the parable is similar in tone to many of the stories Jesus told. It is familiar enough in content, but fails to reveal Jesus as in any sense a Man of Joy. However, the ending of the parable brings us into a totally different situation. The father has been waiting and watching down the road. He sees his boy in the far distance, runs to him, kisses him ardently, and when the young man makes his confession and declares himself unworthy to be his son, the father goes into action.

He calls for the best robe, for a ring and for sandals for his son's feet, and then he orders a calf killed to make a feast. Later the lad's elder brother hears dancing and music in the house. There is no hint that immoral or sinful behavior is involved. Read the text! The father says, "Let us be merry," and so they begin to be merry. When the elder brother protests that the celebration is inappropriate considering the fact that his little brother has "devoured your living with harlots," the father defends his action. "We have to celebrate and make merry," he tells his older son, "because your brother was dead, and is alive; and was lost, and is found."

Let us put to one side all discussion about the parable that is not germane to our search. We want to know what Jesus was like. We want to know if He was as dour and sad as so much Christian art and literature have made Him out to be. The question to be raised in this connection is, Do the joyous scenes at the close of each of these three parables reflect a corresponding joyousness in Jesus' own personality? If they do, the parables tell us something not only about Jesus, but also about His heavenly Father.

Note first that each parable has a happy ending. The same can be said of other parables Jesus told. Even in the parables that ended sadly, Jesus pointed out the things that prevented them from ending happily. He was no misanthrope. If Jesus Himself had not possessed inner joy, He could not have told those stories.

Notice too that in both the first two parables, Heaven and the angels are brought in. The implication is strong: Heaven is a place of celebration. Jesus told us that He came from Heaven.[4]

In another parable which appears in Luke, and also in Matthew and Mark, Jesus uses the figure of the bridegroom to refer to Himself.[5] Here is the entire parable as it appears in Luke.

> They said to Him, "John's disciples often fast and pray, and so do the disciples of the Pharisees, but yours go on eating and drinking."

> Jesus answered, "Can you make the guests of the bridegroom fast while he is with them? But the time will come when the bridegroom will be taken away from them; in those days they will fast."

The concept of Jesus as the bridegroom and the church as the bride is beautifully woven throughout the

Scriptures and through church history as well.[6] It is an honored part of our Christian heritage which we have received with the rest of the divine revelation. However, in this parable Jesus is not discussing the bride; that subject appears later. Now He is referring to the bridegroom and the friends who are helping him celebrate.

A bridegroom is by definition a man of joy. He is filled with eagerness and anticipation. He is one of two principals in a celebration. He is not a lone anchorite fasting in his cell, but a man who is beloved by friends and is about to feast. The recluse in his cell presumably is seeking after holiness, and is utterly sincere in his quest, but the bridegroom in this parable is Himself holiness-haleness-wholeness-joyousness.

Yes, Jesus' disciples were eating and drinking. Yes, they were celebrating because He was with them. What of it? Why shouldn't they? What's wrong with having some joy in life? What is life for, if not for joy? He is the Bridegroom. These are His friends. Yes, they pray, they fast—but not now. Do you get the message?

One of Jesus' best-known stories, recorded in Matthew, is known as the parable of the talents. It is actually a parable of the Kingdom of Heaven. Twice Jesus emphasizes in it that the faithful ones who enter into the Kingdom find the joy of their Lord. In fact, that is the whole point of the parable.[7]

One other brief parable of Jesus needs to be looked at in this context. It is found in Matthew 13:44, and reads as follows: "The kingdom of heaven is like treasure hidden in a field. When a man found it, he hid it again, and then in his joy went and sold all he had and bought that field."

Much can be said, and has been said, to elucidate this parable and to draw spiritual teaching from it. I would like to propose a fresh interpretation. I am suggesting that the treasure was not only the gift of salvation in Christ, but the sheer joy of it. When the man in the field first discovered the treasure he was filled with joy; Jesus made that clear. It was not avarice or greed or covetousness that drove him to sell off everything he owned; it was jubilation. That is the good news of the kingdom Jesus Christ came to share with us; that is what took Him through the agony of torture, crucifixion and death for our sakes. What He came to do, He did for joy, and in doing it He conquered the last enemy, death.[8]

Such is the legacy left to us. In a day when human rights are a universal topic of discussion, here is the greatest of them all: the right to be saved, the right to a new birth, a birthright from God. It is what our Lord Jesus Christ sent the Holy Spirit to bring us, and to foster and sustain in us: unspeakable joy.

❁❁❁

➤ *Questions for Discussion*

1. How do the joyous scenes at the close of each of the parables in Luke 15 reflect a corresponding joyousness in Jesus' own personality?

2. What does Jesus' use of parables and stories in His teaching tell us about the kind of person He was? If you were to meet Him, what would you say to Him?

3. How would you reconcile Jesus' remarks in His parable about the happiness felt by the "bridegroom's friends" with the general condition of the church today as you know it?

11

The Expedition

*Imagine what it would be like if a young
person in our community created uproar
in our local institution for the blind
by making all the residents sighted,
after which he upset the hearing-aid
dispensers by curing deafness.*

As a devotee of the Gilbert and Sullivan oper-
ettas, I've often wondered what it would be like
to rub elbows with those two strange nineteenth-century English gentlemen. I would ask impossible questions such as, Why didn't Sir William Gilbert, as a
person, behave as civilly as the characters he created?
and, Why didn't Sir Arthur Sullivan, who wrote the
music to "Onward Christian Soldiers," draw on the
great biblical themes for his serious compositions
instead of orchestrating all those tiresome old legends?

But trying to project myself into the milieu of a hundred years ago has proved extremely difficult.

If the nineteenth century seems so remote after the passage of a mere century, how much more difficult it is to imagine oneself back in the days of the Roman Empire. When I tour the Holy Land I easily recognize some of the ancient landmarks, but I cannot honestly say that I walked where Jesus walked. Too much time has passed; too many wars have scarred the topography. The Romans have gone, and so have the Babylonians, the Assyrians, the Egyptians, the Parthians, the Arabians, the Crusaders, the Saracens, the Turks, the Syrians, the French, the British, and the rest. The task I have set in this chapter therefore is not easy, but it must be tackled.

Our expedition of discovery into the Gospels will attempt to bring to the surface the basic reason for the joy and excitement that surrounded Jesus during His itinerant ministry. Much of the Gospel narrative as it stands is taken up with conflict—and rightly so, for our Lord had a mission to carry out, and it drew opposition from the start. But apart from all the controversies with officialdom, secular and religious, we will I believe also find hints that the effect Jesus had upon the population as a whole was nothing short of sensational.

All we have to do, really, is to imagine what it would be like if a young person in our community created uproar in our local institution for the blind by making all the residents sighted; after which he upset the hearing-aid dispensers by curing deafness, and caused consternation in the physiotherapy clinics by restoring paralyzed limbs to normal functioning; then confused the interment crews in the nearby cemetery by bringing back to life corpses on their way to the gravesite; displayed uncanny knowledge of the location and habits of freshwater fish; fed thousands of homeless persons with no visible food supply beyond a couple of hamburgers; calmed a storm on one of the Great Lakes by day and walked on its surface by night.

There is little doubt that not only would such a person immediately attract enormous attention from the county sheriff and television news cameras, but also that a crowd would speedily gather and either applaud or start picketing his movements.

John tells us that a young man blind from birth received his sight at the hands of Jesus.[1] Can you imagine his not being transported with joy? Luke relates that when Jesus interrupted a funeral procession in the village of Nain and restored a dead youth alive to his mother, the crowd at the town gate was stunned at first. Then after the truth of what happened became known, the response of the people was electric. Shouts of "Hallelujah!" were heard, and an atmosphere of celebration pervaded the country-side. Friends whispered to each other in awe, "God has visited His people!"[2]

Luke tells us further that beginning at His home in Nazareth, Jesus went through the countryside city by city and village by village, giving out "the glad tidings of the kingdom of God."[3] In each place multitudes assembled to hear "the gracious words proceeding from his mouth." People brought gifts to Him. Matthew writes that similar crowds followed Him throughout Galilee and that He "healed all the sick."[4] What a stupendous outpouring of elation and affection must have accompanied those healing events!

In Jericho, when Bartimaeus was healed of blindness and began to glorify God, Luke says that all the people saw it, and they joined in praising the Lord.[5] When Jesus straightened up the backbone of a woman who had been bent over by her infirmity for eighteen years, "all his opponents were humiliated, but the people were delighted with all the wonderful things he was doing."[6] Again, what bursts of joy and enthusiasm those events must have caused! What shouting! What singing! Yes, what leaping! Small wonder that, as Mark says in the New King James translation, "The common people heard Him gladly."[7]

Never before nor since in the history of the human race has there been anything to match the ministry of the Man from Nazareth. He was the Life-Changer, the Master of His environment, the Paragon of good works, and the most wonderful part of it was that in all those mighty deeds He said He was simply executing the perfect will of His heavenly Father.[8]

What effect did this dazzling display of love and joy have on those who came after Jesus? Was there a carryover among His followers in the days and years that succeeded His time on earth? It is a vital question for us in our time, for we too bear His name. We too want to be numbered among "the saints" when they "go marching in." We claim to be "followers of the Way" in this generation, and if it turned out that Jesus' own intimate disciples failed to unlock His secret, we might as well ask what prospect for joy there is for us poor pilgrims as we plod into a dangerous new millennium.

Jesus was specific in telling His disciples it was His intent that "my joy may be in you and that your joy may be complete."[9] Even when He informed them of His approaching death, He specifically added, "Now is your time of grief, but I will see you again and you will rejoice, and no one will take away your joy."[10]

To continue on our expedition, let us see how some of the disciples reacted to the news of Jesus' resurrection on the first day of the week. As might be expected, disbelief was prevalent among them at first, even after the empty tomb had been examined. Soon however attitudes changed dramatically. Luke gives us a fascinating account of what happened to two disciples, Cleopas and another (his wife?) on their journey that same afternoon from Jerusalem to their home in Emmaus, seven miles away.[11]

It seems that while the two disciples were walking on the road, Jesus, the risen Lord traveling incognito, drew alongside and greeted them. He asked them what they had been conversing about and (please note particularly) why their faces were so gloomy? (The inference could be that Jesus Himself was at the time anything but gloomy; that He was in fact in a rapturous state of elation!)

Not recognizing who the stranger was, the two disciples told Him of the tragic events that had just taken place in Jerusalem, and added they had also heard that some women had found Jesus' tomb empty and that they claimed they had a vision of angels who told them He was alive.

Jesus answered them with an expression that our translators render as "O fools!" or "O senseless ones!"[12]

But if Jesus was truly in a state of resurrection joy, could not He have had a smile on His wonderful face as He said it? Could it not have come out as something like, "You missed it!" He told them they were "slow of heart" to accept the prophetic writings, which sounds as if He were saying to them, "You're not using your heads!" Then He proceeded to explain His Father's whole plan of redemption, beginning with Moses and the prophets and ending with His own suffering in Jerusalem and His now imminent departure for the realms of glory and everlasting joy.

How effective Jesus' teaching was during that long walk may be gathered from what the two disciples said later: "Didn't He set our hearts afire as He opened the Scriptures to us on the way?"[13]

When they reached Emmaus it was late in the day, and the two invited their new friend to join them (in their home?) for supper. Jesus seems to have intended to go on, but He accepted their offer of hospitality and stayed. They spread a table for supper, and then the excitement really began.

Jesus assumed the role of host, even though He was a guest. He took the loaf of bread before Him, offered thanks to God, then broke it and gave it to the disciples. In that moment the veil dropped from their eyes and they knew Him. And then, Luke tells us, Jesus disappeared. Like that. There He was, reclining at table with them, and then He wasn't.

Immediately the two disciples rose to their feet, and within minutes they were out the door and on their way back to Jerusalem. It must have been some trip! They went in the dark without street lights, flashlights, or any kind of lights except, possibly, a pine torch or a moon overhead. Certainly there were bandits abroad. Whatever the difficulties, they made it back to the city and to where the eleven disciples were gathered.

The record doesn't tell us so, but we can assume that the gloom was gone from the faces of those two disciples. They had found the secret!

John tells us that the other disciples were meeting at the same time in Jerusalem in a room with locked doors, when Jesus appeared among them. He showed them the wounds on His hands and feet, and John says, "The disciples were overjoyed when they saw the Lord."[14] Not just impressed, or pleased, or glad—"overjoyed."

Let me ask you candidly, how would you have felt if you had been there? If you had watched Jesus eating a piece of broiled fish only three days after you had beheld Him hanging dead on a cross,[15] how would you have reacted? Would you have been terrified? Would you have sat there with a long, sober face, shaking your head? Or would you have started celebrating the way you did when your team finally won the Super Bowl or the World Cup?

We come now to a highly significant scene. Some days have passed since the meeting in the locked room and other resurrection appearances have occurred. We find Jesus presently leading His disciples in a southerly direction over the gentle crest of the Mount of Olives to a spot near the village of Bethany. There, while He is in the act of blessing them, He is taken up into Heaven, and a cloud obscures Him from their vision. A man, a real man, a sinless man unlike any other human being since the dawn of creation, a Person of transcendent joy, has left the earth.

How do the disciples react? With cries of dismay and much weeping? No. Luke tells us that two men "in white apparel" stood by and quietly reminded them that Jesus would be returning.[16] That was what they wanted to hear. Did they engage in a "solemn act of worship," as Dean Alford suggests?[17] Look at the test. That the disciples worshiped Jesus is clear, but Luke's Gospel tells us that they then returned to Jerusalem "with great joy" and were "continually at the temple, praising God."[18] You decide what kind of worship it was.

On the day of Pentecost the band of believers was still celebrating the resurrection of their Lord in Jerusalem. The joy of the disciples was so pronounced that bystanders made fun of them and said, "It must be the wine."[19]

The apostle Peter however rose to the occasion. Addressing the crowd, he said not so; it was only 9 o'clock in the morning, and this was a fulfillment of Joel's prophecy that a day was coming when God would pour out His Spirit upon the people.[20]

After one has attended a long, reserved, dignified, formal ceremony in one of our hoary and venerable old churches, is it not a relief to emerge from that "dim religious light"[21] into the natural brightness of God's sunshine? I cannot imagine a sharper contrast when one compares such solemnity with the New Testament's description of the first Pentecost. Am I assuming that the occasion was more joyous than the text in the Book of Acts warrants? We are told that Peter preached a sermon in which he quoted from the Psalms, and this was what he chose:

> My heart is glad and my tongue rejoices;
>   my body also will live in hope . . .
> You have made known to me the paths of life;
>   You will fill me with joy in your presence.[22]

A baptism followed the preaching, and three thousand persons were added to the number of believers. Quite a celebration!

The Book of Acts also records that in the days following Pentecost the new Christians "broke bread in their homes and ate together with glad and sincere hearts, praising God and enjoying the favor of all the people."[23] Of course. The people saw the joy, and once they were convinced it was real, many of them decided it was what they wanted for themselves. "And the Lord added to their number daily those who were being saved."[24] Of course. Why not?

The apostle Philip visited a city in Samaria where he preached the Gospel of Christ. The crowds came, people were converted and healed, and "there was great joy in that city."[25] Some days later he touched the life of a distinguished African gentleman, baptized him, and the man went back to Ethiopia full of joy.[26]

Even flogging failed to shake the jubilant spirits of the apostles. When Paul and Barnabas were expelled from Antioch of Pisidia, they left behind non-Jewish disciples, new converts who "were filled with joy and with the Holy Spirit."[27]

When the two missionaries reached Lystra, a hilarious scene occurred after Paul was used to heal a man with crippled feet. Lystra being a city devoted to the pagan Greek gods, the people decided that Barnabas was actually Zeus in human form, and Paul was Hermes, the supposed messenger of the gods. The temple priest ordered bulls and garlands brought to the city gates and encouraged the crowd to offer sacrifices to the men. Barnabas and Paul were hard put to prove their humanity but in doing so, they preached the good news of the kingdom, and told the Lycaonians that God not only provided them with seasonal rains and food, but he also "fills your hearts with joy."[28] That made the people even more eager to sacrifice to them.

Later, when Paul and Silas sailed across to Macedonia to plant the Gospel in Europe, they ran into fresh opposition and soon found themselves in a jail in Philippi. At midnight they were wide awake, replete with the joy of the Spirit, filling the dank prison air with psalms and hymns and spiritual songs which edified and no doubt entertained the other prisoners. What joy! What dauntless spirits! These two men had been whipped only a few hours earlier, yet here they were, exhibiting an invincible quality of life that was characteristic of our Lord Jesus Christ Himself.

Why is it that the scholars and savants (some of whom claim that Paul had no sense of humor) miss the light touch that keeps reappearing throughout the Book of Acts?

Think again of Paul and Silas in the Philippian jail, singing praises in the darkness of that chamber of horrors. When an earthquake shook the jail into rubble, and the jailer was about to kill himself, Paul and Silas told him to stop, that nobody was trying to escape. The jailer was so impressed by their attitude that he asked them how he could be saved. They told him. How they told him! He was convinced, converted and baptized, and before the night was over the jailer had fed Paul and Silas and attended to their wounds which he, possibly, had ordered inflicted. And how did the jailer feel about his demolished calaboose? We don't know. How did his family feel about the earthquake? We don't know that either. All we are told is that the whole family was filled with joy because they had come to believe in God.[29]

If that were not enough, when morning came and the city magistrate ordered Paul and Silas released, they refused to go without an official escort. They announced that they were Roman citizens, which exempted them from brutality and harassment by the local constabulary. A beautiful touch. The bureaucracy panicked, an official escort was dispatched to the jail, and as Halford Luccock expressed it, "with sore backs and heads held high" (and no doubt with smiles on their faces) the two ambassadors of the Lord strode out through the broken prison gates of Philippi and into the chronicles of history.[30]

To be sure, nearly everywhere Paul took the Gospel, whether to Pisidian Antioch, Iconium, Lystra, Thessalonica, Berea, Corinth, Ephesus or Jerusalem, uproar resulted. Yet the man himself seemed to be in the eye of the hurricane, untroubled in spirit. "Keep up your courage," he told the half-drowned sailors aboard the floundering ship on which he was a prisoner. "Get something to eat. You're going to survive, all of you."[31]

On the island of Malta, when a poisonous snake bit him on the hand, he casually shook it off into the fire.[32] When he reached Italy, he was met by a delegation of Christians who had traveled forty-three miles from Rome to greet him at the marketplace of Appius; Paul's response was to give thanks to God and take courage.[33]

In a letter to the Christians of Corinth Paul expressed his feelings and those of his companions well:

> We are hard pressed on every side, but not crushed; perplexed, but not in despair; persecuted, but not abandoned; struck down, but not destroyed. We always carry around in our body the death of Jesus, so that the life of Jesus may also be revealed in our body . . . [we are] sorrowful, yet always rejoicing . . . In all our troubles my joy knows no bounds."[34]

Joy! It is the one key word that distinguishes the authentic Paul from all the spurious letters attributed to him in the early centuries of the Christian era. Paul wrote again and again of his joy; his imitators did not.

Finally, when word of the conversions among the Greeks of Asia Minor was carried to the Christians in

Phoenicia and Samaria, the Book of Acts states that "the news made all the brothers very glad."[35]

Our expeditionary search has been rewarded. We have found ample evidence of the jubilant, animating principle which characterized Jesus' early ministry and the joy and excitement that welcomed and surrounded it. We are also assured that that principle of jubilation survived the tragic events in Jerusalem, that Pentecost brought a fresh touch of joy to the young church, and that the disciples and apostles were able to carry their Master's secret with them on their evangelistic journeys.

❂❂❂

➤ Questions for Discussion

1. Jesus said that His purpose was "that my joy may be in you and that your joy may be complete." How would you say that such a purpose was conveyed to and fulfilled in His disciples?

2. Would you say that His purpose is being carried out in the church today? How?

3. Is it realistic to "count it all joy" as the Letter of James expresses it? Can we assume that we are able to experience joy in the midst of our trials and disappointments? How is this done?

12

Poets and Prophets

*Perhaps the joy of our salvation
so evident in the New Testament
is being felt once again
in some of our churches.*

Throughout the past several chapters I have bombarded the reader with questions: If the Bible is so full of joy, and Bibles are everywhere today, where is the joy? And if the Gospel really is glad tidings, who is preaching it? And if Jesus Christ was and is truly a Man of joy, why is He usually represented otherwise?

In this chapter we will look for answers by going back to the only Bible that Jesus knew, namely, the

Old Testament. Jesus loved this ancient Hebrew document, which has provided such an inexhaustible supply of inspiration to the human race. Nothing in literature can compare with it. We shall be looking at certain sacred books that relate directly to our subject.

The Psalms we have already examined briefly, noting that the words *gladness, joyousness, delight* and *jubilation* appear some 108 times in these immortal poems—which may help explain why the Psalms are the most popular of all Judeo-Christian writings.

But now let us turn our attention to the Book of Isaiah the prophet. In these sixty-six chapters may be found passages of exalted expression that are unmatched in sacred writings. It is not our present purpose to analyze them poetically, prophetically, grammatically or historically, even if we could. We shall simply look for the joy. Here are some excerpts:

"Surely God is my salvation;
  I will trust and not be afraid.
The LORD, the LORD, is my strength and my song;
  He has become my salvation."
With joy you will draw water
  from the wells of salvation.

The wilderness and the wasteland
  shall be glad for them,
And the desert shall rejoice and
  blossom as the meadow saffron;
It shall blossom abundantly and rejoice. . . .
They will enter Zion with singing;
  everlasting joy will crown their heads.
Gladness and joy will overtake them,
  and sorrow and sighing will flee away.

I will make you the everlasting pride
  and the joy of all generations.

He has sent me . . . to bestow on them a crown of
    beauty
  instead of ashes,
the oil of gladness
  instead of mourning,
and a garment of praise
  instead of a spirit of despair . . .
and so they will inherit a double portion in their land,
  and everlasting joy will be theirs.

For I will create Jerusalem to be a delight
  and its people a joy.[1]

Small wonder Isaiah's prophecies have been popularly linked with the Psalms as the two favorite portions of the Old Testament for more than twenty-five hundred years. The songs Isaiah sings are messianic, and they are so packed with joyful promise that they fill the believer's heart with longing for the coming of the Lord. The joys of the faithful are always tied to the glorious future God has prepared for those who love Him.

The Book of Proverbs mentions the words joy, gladness and delight thirty-one times by my count. Because of their nature, the sayings are brief and to the point. Here are some examples:

The LORD . . . delights in men who are truthful.

The cheerful [merry] heart has a continual feast.

A cheerful heart is good medicine.

When justice is done, it brings joy to the righteous.

When the righteous triumph, there is great elation.

He who has a wise son delights in him.

Perfume and incense bring joy to the heart,
  and the pleasantness of one's friend springs from
    his earnest counsel.[2]

One of the most beautiful passages in Proverbs is not a proverb at all, but a poetic soliloquy personified and placed in the mouth of Wisdom. In describing the work of the Creator as He shaped the heavens and the earth, Wisdom concludes:

> Then I was the craftsman at His side.
> I was filled with delight day after day,
>   rejoicing always in His presence,
> rejoicing in His whole world
>   and delighting in mankind.[3]

In the Book of the Prophet Jeremiah, the Hebrew equivalents of joy, delight and gladness appear twenty-eight times.

> When your words came, I ate them;
>   they were my joy and my heart's delight.

> I am the LORD, who exercises kindness,
>   justice and righteousness on earth,
>   for in these I delight.[4]

When one bears in mind that traditionally Jeremiah is known as the "weeping prophet" (due in large part to his connection with the Book of Lamentations that follows his prophecy), these joyful passages, predicting the forthcoming deliverance of the Jewish people from their Babylonian captivity, are all the more significant:

> For the LORD will ransom Jacob . . .
> They will come and shout for joy on the heights of
>   Zion;
>   they will rejoice in the bounty of the Lord . . .
> They will be like a well-watered garden,
>   and they will sorrow no more.
> Then maidens will dance and be glad,
>   young men and old as well.
> I will turn their mourning into gladness;
>   I will give them comfort and joy instead of sorrow.[5]

Such is the word of the Lord to one of the greatest prophets of all time, a man whose name has been expropriated to coin a word for mournful complaining—the *jeremiad.*

The most beautiful Old Testament expressions of transport and delight, however, are found not in the prophets but in the poets—more specifically in the Song of Songs which is Solomon's. (For reasons that shall appear, I shall follow the NIV in referring to it as the Song of Songs.)

Here, embedded in the ancient Hebrew canon, is undoubtedly the most exquisite love poem ever written. Like another magnificent poem, the Book of Job, it is hidden in the midst of other Old Testament books which recount the wars, massacres, assassinations, invasions, sufferings and starvation of the Hebrew tribes and their neighbors, all of which are accompanied by warnings and predictions of judgment and wrath to come. Of course divine sorrow and anguish over sin are expressed throughout the Old Testament. Such expressions fulfill a prophetic role and have an honored place in the oracles of God. Jesus as the Messiah stood in the noble tradition of the prophets of Israel. He warned His generation in the strongest possible terms of the consequences of its unjust and sinful behavior and the fate of all evildoers.

This present book is an attempt however to look at the other side of the Bible, the neglected side, the side of unparalleled beauty and bliss, the side of joy and laughter. Forgive me if in the zeal of my effort to redress the imbalance, I seem to stray from the path of knowledge and lean too far.

The Song of Songs is a love poem. The reader should pause at this point, lay down the book in his or her hands, pick up the Bible and read the eight short chapters of the Song, which is primarily a beautiful exchange between two lovers. Until one has absorbed the Song verse by verse, in all its exotic and erotic flavor and mysterious references, one cannot fully appreciate what it has to do with joy.

The Song of Songs has been called the most obscure book in the Bible.[6] Early Christian commentators (Origen and Jerome) quote a Jewish saying that no one should study the Song until he (or she) has reached thirty years of age. Goethe called it the most divine of all love songs. Franz Delitzsch, the great German scholar, says, "No other book of Scripture has been so much abused by an unscientific spiritualizing and an over-scientific unspiritual treatment."[7]

The Song is not scientific at all. It is a dramatic pastoral, a sunny interchange, a joyous dialogue between a bridegroom and his bride. It radiates expressions of warm affection, using the imagery of flowers and fruits, gardens and perfumes, wind and water, fields and mountains, spices and jewelry. While the transitions are not always easy to follow, the total effect is enchanting.

Today Christian and Jewish marriage counselors are using the Song of Songs to break down barriers between couples, barriers that are keeping husbands and wives from fully expressing their love for each other.[8] It is reported to be highly effective.

Ever since the rabbis received it into the Bible, the Song of Songs has been a subject of controversy. The language is so sensuous, and the role of Shulamith, the woman, is so obviously and completely equal in importance to that of her lover that the book could only be accepted into the ancient Jewish culture by regarding it as an allegory. King Solomon, it was decided, was God, the lover, and Shulamith, the beloved young lady, was the people of Israel. Accordingly, the subject of the Song was held to be Israel's history from the Exodus until the future coming of the Messiah.

So much for the Jewish view of the Song of Songs. The church in turn accepted the poem allegorically, but the early Christian writers changed the *dramatis personae.* The lover and his beloved became symbols of Jesus Christ and His church. According to this interpretation, King Solomon represented Christ, while Shulamith was the holy bride, the beloved, the chosen elect of the Lord. This view is still popular in Christian circles and is not without its validity, but it fails to reveal to us how the poem came to be composed in the first place. Sensuous love poems are not usually written for religious reasons.

On its face, the Song of Songs is simply a rare and unforgettable paean of joy, a passionate, tender, rapturous, human expression of love between a young man and a young woman. In the hands of early theologians it became something much more mysterious and complex.

Origen wrote twelve volumes to elaborate his religious interpretations of the Song.

Bernard of Clairvaux, a twelfth century monk famous for his hymns and devotional writings, preached eighty-six sermons on the "Canticles," as they were called, and when he died, he had reached only the end of the second chapter.[9]

Ernst Hengstenberg, an otherwise reputable German evangelical scholar, carried his allegorical interpretation of the Song of Songs to such lengths that he declared the "rounded navel" of the lovely Shulamith "denotes the cup from which the church refreshes those that thirst for salvation with a noble and refreshing draught."[10] (Who says textual scholars don't have a sense of humor?)

Certain passages in the Song of Songs have genuinely stirred me to a closer personal relationship with Christ. To cite just two:

> I am a rose of Sharon,
>   a lily of the valleys . . .
> He has taken me to the banquet hall,
>   and His banner over me is love.[11]

It is not my purpose to impeach the work of Christian scholars in their efforts to "spiritualize" the Song of Songs. However, I am convinced that the only natural interpretation of the Song is to acknowledge it to be what one Christian counselor has described as a "joyous celebration of sacred married love."[12]

> How beautiful you are and how pleasing,
>   O love, with your delights!
>
> Show me your face,
>   let me hear your voice,
> for your voice is sweet,
>   and your face is lovely.
>
> You have stolen my heart, my sister, my bride;
>   you have stolen my heart
> with one glance of your eyes.[13]

No wonder that on the day of his wedding the lover's heart was enraptured!

The joy that the two lovers knew in the Song of Songs is just another facet of the jewel that is the gospel treasure. In the Christian view, true love between husband and wife draws its richness, its beauty and its joy from the love that Jesus brought from Heaven to share with His friends. That love, when it is planted in the human heart, brings with it the joy of life everlasting, the gift of God Himself. It is a holy thing, but no less delightful because it is holy, and it is certainly what God intended for Christians—and Christian marriage.

One commentator, R. A. Redford, says, "No one can accept the Song of Solomon as a book of Scripture . . . without forming some theory of interpretation which shall justify the position of such a book among the sacred writings."[14]

Before leaving this delectable poem with its garden of delights, I would like to add my own theory. I claim no special qualification for offering it except the word of Jesus: "Out of the overflow of the heart the mouth speaks."[15]

I believe the Song of Songs was written to King Solomon by someone living during his reign. I believe that the song was neither by Solomon nor about him. Rather it is a dramatic love colloquy between a shepherd and a country girl, who use the imagery of royalty to address and describe each other in fantasy.

To the Shulamite girl, chaste and beautiful, her young lover appears like King Solomon in all his majesty. She sees him wearing a crown, riding in a chariot and escorted by warriors. This is her man, "her own Solomon, her own special king," as Professor Hugh T. Kerr expresses it,[16] and she probably infinitely prefers him to the fabulously wealthy king who is such a prolific lover of women. Yet in her romantic mind she adores the royal trappings.

The young shepherd on his part imagines his beloved as a prince's daughter, spreading her perfume at the royal table, admired by queens and surrounded by the "daughters of Jerusalem." In his fantasy she is as fair as the moon, bright as the sun, and majestic as troops with banners. Among the ladies she is herself the queen.

King Solomon, his retinue, his horses and chariots become in this Song nothing but the sweet word pictures and imaginative expressions that lovers use. Once we see that, the puzzle is solved. All the vexing questions, such as how and where the girl from the vineyards of Galilee could fit into the dazzling atmosphere of the royal palace as the king's lover (along with the hundreds of wives and concubines), and how Solomon could double as a country sheepherder, are laid to rest. For lovers have always used the language of the royal court in their most intimate conversations, sometimes in play, sometimes in passion. We may say to our spouse in such secluded moments, "You're my prince! You're my sovereign lord!" Or, "You're my queen! You're my royal princess!" In past centuries the monks who wrote interminable sermons about the Canticles may not have understood such endearments; but we do.

In a sermon he preached in Solomon's colonnade, recorded in the third chapter of the Book of Acts, Peter speaks of a time coming when God will restore everything.[17] Perhaps it is a welcome sign of the early return of our Lord that the human element is being restored today to the Song of Songs. We can now read and enjoy it as it was originally composed, with all the unnecessary religious symbolism and allegorizing peeled away.

Perhaps what is happening to this love poem is also happening in our generation to the Gospel of Jesus Christ itself, and the joy of our salvation that is so evident in the New Testament is being felt once again in some of our churches. Perhaps the artificial solemnity and ponderous religious severity that has accompanied so much of our divine worship in a minor key is being lifted, so that we can begin to praise God as the psalmist did, not with subduedness but with gladness of heart and fullness of joy.

Yet with all the thrill of finding new meanings in the ancient Word, we should never forget the classic description of the church contained in the Book of Revelation: "I saw the Holy City, the new Jerusalem, coming down out of Heaven from God, prepared as a bride beautifully dressed for her husband."[18] Christians who know their Bible believe that one day Jesus' promise to return for His church, expressed in John 14:2, will be fulfilled. And with what words will He address His own? Perhaps the words of the Song of Songs:

> Come away, my lover,
>   and be like a gazelle
>   or like a young stag
>   on the spice-laden mountains.[19]

❀❀❀

➤ *Questions for Discussion*

1. Why do you think the church allegorized the Song of Solomon instead of accepting it as it is?

2. How would you say the Song of Songs can help married couples today in their personal relationships?

3. What evidence have you seen of a warming trend in the churches today? Has it reached you?

13

Amazing Grace

It is in the eye of a child, the trill of a meadowlark, the touch of a lover, the opening bars of the "Moonlight Sonata" . . .

At this point it is possible we have enough evidence to say that Jesus came to earth on a joyous mission of salvation, and that one of His aims was that others might share that joy. Many people I have talked with acknowledge Jesus as the Author and Finisher of their faith, but they are wondering whether they might not have been missing something in their Christian lives. If Jesus had a secret, they don't know what it is. As for the New Testament's strong emphasis upon joy, they admit it didn't come through to them; they thought it was just preacher talk.

The time has come to say bluntly regarding this joy, "It sounds great if it's true," and then ask, "Where do we get it?"

To find out, we need to look at Jesus' mission. He came with orders to bring redemption to the human race, to draw men and women back to God, and to usher in His Kingdom. After His baptism in the river Jordan He came into Galilee from the desert joyously, fresh from His victory over Satan, filled with the power of the Holy Spirit, and He launched His ministry on a high note. "The time has come," He announced. "The Kingdom of God is near. Repent and believe the Good News!"[1]

This was uttered by no stern-faced prophet of doom. This was an elated, triumphant young Man saying, "Come! Join me! I know the way out of this. There is a good life, a great life. Take it from Me. Everything is ready. Come!"

And they did come, by the hundreds and thousands. But as we note the euphoria that accompanied that magnificent ministry, we dare not lose sight of the fact that Jesus came to earth at His Father's behest and accomplished His earthly mission only with the supreme sacrifice of His own life. By dying upon the cross at Calvary and bearing our sins in His own body, Jesus removed the barrier between us and our Maker, and opened the gates of Heaven to all who believe in Him.

The shedding of His blood upon the cross was not precipitated by mere action on the part of others. Jesus made it abundantly clear that His sacrifice was not intended to appease an angry deity; rather it was His own personal decision to carry out the work His beloved Father had commissioned Him to do.[2] "God was in Christ reconciling the world to Himself."[3] As the late Reuben Torrey so well expressed it:

> In the atoning death of His Son, instead of laying the punishment of guilty man upon an innocent third person, God took the shame and suffering due

to man upon Himself; and so far from that being unjust and cruel, it is amazing grace![4]

At one time in my life I had to face two questions: Did Jesus die for me? And if He did, why did He? Since Sunday school days I had admired Jesus, but only recently had such questions begun to press me. While in uniform during World War II I picked up a devotional booklet written by a Jewish army chaplain. He was explaining the Passover to Jewish troops and he used words like these: "You will discover in life that the innocent must suffer for the guilty. Such is the way to peace. But instead of it being all wrong, it is the answer to everything. The secret of life is sacrifice."

To illustrate, he pointed to the young troops who did not create international quarrels but were being sent into combat to settle them. "To understand that," he said, "is to know the deeper meaning of existence."

I thought of Jesus. He was innocent, yet He was said to have suffered and died for the guilty. I felt this chaplain was on the track of something. I was a sinner. Jesus went to the cross, the innocent for the guilty—or so they said. It was, it seemed, the only way my sins could be forgiven. But did that mean Jesus actually took my place, that there had been a substitution?

It was evident there were some things I could not do for myself. I have never forgotten an occasion in the Aleutian islands when two soldiers went to my commanding officer without my knowledge to defend my actions, for I was in trouble. They went on my behalf and took my place. Their kindness lingers in my memory as a sweet fragrance.

I was willing to grant that perhaps in some symbolic way Jesus died on my behalf; that He saw His role as that of a Messiah who would lay down His life for others in a kind of vicarious sacrifice.

What I couldn't see was why He would do it for me. In fact, I couldn't fathom why Jesus or anyone else would want to die for me. I told myself I was quite ready to take the rap for my shortcomings. I preferred to settle my own accounts, thank you very much.

A few years later a remarkable book made its appearance. It was a commentary on the Gospel of John by Arthur John Gossip, a Scottish preacher whom I had once heard and whom I deeply respected. I had read his other books and reveled in his wide learning and eloquent prose. I considered him a worthy man of God.

As I read Dr. Gossip's exposition of John, the old questions came back, still haunting: *Did Jesus die for me? And if He did, why did He?* I had reached the eighteenth chapter of the Gospel, which tells of Pilate's offer to the crowd to release Jesus, since one prisoner was customarily set free at the Passover season. The crowd responded that they preferred the release of another prisoner named Barabbas rather than Jesus.

At this point Dr. Gossip observed:

> With reason and truth scholars keep pointing out that when the Scriptures tell us that Christ died for us, the [Greek] preposition used [means] "on behalf of," and not "in the place of." For Barabbas at least there was no such distinction. And it is never clean cut. "On behalf of" keeps merging into "in the place of," do what you will.

Dr. Gossip then paid tribute to the British army troops with whom he served in France during World War I, saying that . . .

those who laid down their lives there, did it for us, on our behalf. That certainly. That undeniably. But many feel that even that is an inadequate account of what they did and what we owe them, that they bore and died not merely upon our behalf but literally in our stead.

In conclusion Dr. Gossip quoted Dr. James Denney, another noted Scottish theologian of the early twentieth century:

> What then is it which we are spared or saved from by the death of Jesus—what is it we do not experience because He died? The answer is that He saves us from dying in our sins. But for His death, we should have died in our sins; we should have passed into the blackness of darkness with the condemnation of God abiding on us. It is because He died for us, and for no other reason, that the darkness has passed away, and a light shines in which we have peace with God and rejoice in hope of His glory.[5]

Since I read those words I have never again had problems with what the theologians call the "substitutionary atonement of Jesus Christ." The Holy Spirit has swept all my doubts off the lee side of the deck and they have never blown back. I believe that Jesus Christ took my sins upon Himself and died for me because He loved me and wanted me to be in Heaven with Him. When a preacher says, "God said it, Christ did it, I believe it, that settles it," I now add, "Amen. Hallelujah!"

That answer, however, does not take care of the question raised earlier in this chapter: Where do we get the joy? If it be true that we cannot have the joy without the salvation, it seems to be equally true that many who have the salvation have missed out to a large extent on the joy.

So how do we get it?

The answer of Scripture is that joy is a fruit of the Holy Spirit. Fruit comes from abiding in the Vine. Jesus is the Vine. When the fruit is ripe it is plucked, but we don't grow it, God grows it; and we don't pluck it, others do. As John implies, we pass on the joy and share it.

Thus joy is not something we do, but something we receive and to which we respond. It is a gift of grace through the Holy Spirit.

A whole new area of thought now opens before us. What exactly is grace? The song "Amazing Grace" is extremely popular; it gives insight into what grace does, but does not really define it. The quick explanation of most Christians is, "Grace is unmerited favor," and perhaps that statement should be our starting point.

Grace is indeed something coming to us that we don't deserve. Not that we don't want it, or covet it, or pray for it, or anticipate it, or expect it, or try to earn points toward it, or strain and perspire after it. The whole point and meaning of grace is that we can't and don't do anything to warrant receiving it. It comes to us out of the blue, a free gift dropped in our laps, so to speak.

Here is a clumsy illustration: Suppose to help out a worthy cause you purchase a ticket in a drawing. You forget about it and it turns out (as it always does) that someone else won the prize. But wait. Suppose some other person, a stranger perhaps, buys a ticket in another drawing without your knowledge, walks up to you on the street, and graciously hands it to you. A miracle happens and its number comes up. You are the winner! This is not an example of grace, but it does illustrate perhaps how grace works. It is favor unearned, undeserved, and often unexpected.

I told you I didn't want Jesus to die for me. He did it anyway. The grace of God, then, is something that comes by the Holy Spirit without our initiating it, or causing it, or even fully understanding it; and the joy of our salvation is something that comes by grace.

Grace has a powerful theological meaning that is the centerpiece of all that Christians believe. We are saved by grace. But the word has other meanings as well.

Here are some of the definitions the dictionary gives for grace: an attractive quality or endowment; good will; love; mercy; clemency; leniency; pardon; moral strength; kindness; attractiveness; esteem; beauty; charm; benignity.

It is not hard to associate joy with these qualities, but the reason joy is part of grace is not because grace is such a pleasant word. It is because grace comes from the hand of the Creator, without any effort on our side. It is like the sunshine; we didn't put it there, but we accept it thankfully, bask in it, use it, flourish and glory in it. Joy being wrapped up in the gift of God's grace, all we have to do is reach out and take it.

Actually it's everywhere. It is in the eye of a child, the trill of a meadowlark, the flight of a crane, the smile of a sleeping infant, the twinkle in the eye of a grandparent, the touch of a lover, the somersaults of a sea otter, the opening bars of the "Moonlight Sonata," the hug of a lost teenager who has come home . . .

> . . . a sunset touch,
> A fancy from a flower-bell . . .
> A chorus-ending from Euripedes . . . [6]

and the passing of one of God's beloved into the holy Presence.

Joy is there for the taking, and if you wish to grasp it, open your Bible to the one-hundredth Psalm and start to read. And may the amazing grace of our Lord Jesus Christ and the touch of His ineffable joy be upon your spirit.

❁❁❁

➤ *Questions for Discussion*

1. If the Holy Spirit is love, what does it mean to you to be filled with the Spirit, and what does it mean not to be filled with the Spirit?

2. Discuss how it is possible for a person to become a Christian and to live an active Christian life without experiencing the joy that Jesus and the early disciples knew.

3. What is the relationship between the Holy Spirit, the grace of God, and joy in the life of the believer? (Cf. Romans 5:5.)

14

Man of Sorrows

When Christians speak of Jesus as a
'Man of Sorrows' who is 'acquainted with
grief,' they are not describing
His inner spiritual nature.

In his first letter to believers in Asia, the apostle
Peter waxes eloquent about the mercy of God,
the new birth, the raising of Jesus from the dead, and
the marvelous inheritance of joy that awaits the believer in Heaven. We read those inspired words and
think, "What a glorious prospect! What an exciting
thing to be a Christian!"

Then Peter drops the other shoe. Unfortunately,
he adds, just now for a little while there will be trials,
grief and suffering.[1]

That, in a capsule, is where we are.

According to the Gospel of Mark, even before He began His ministry Jesus had encountered His first opposition. His adversary was Satan, whom He met in the desert.[2] Shortly afterward Jesus returned to Galilee and healed a paralyzed man, telling him his sins were forgiven.[3] Jesus thereby raised up some human opposition, which increased after He ate a meal with some questionable characters and performed a healing on the Sabbath.[4] By the beginning of the third chapter of Mark, Jesus' enemies were plotting to get rid of him.[5]

From our frontier days comes a saying that when you are up to your neck in alligators, it's hard to keep your mind on the fact that you're there to drain the swamp. When people are following you, hounding you, and trying to entrap you, it's hard to maintain a serene countenance of joy. And when you are trying to clear commercial vendors out of a holy sanctuary, it's hard to exude a spirit of good will.

Jesus found Himself in trouble, not from the people as a whole, but from the "keepers of the Law" who considered themselves God's monitors of social behavior. Over the next three years they sought to turn the Man of Joy into a Man of Sorrows. There is a sense in which the title "Man of Sorrows" properly and appropriately applies to Jesus. It is a messianic title, and Jesus in fulfilling His Father's will unquestionably assumed the prophetic role so movingly described in Isaiah 53.

Yet when Christians speak of Jesus as a "Man of Sorrows" who is "acquainted with grief," they are not describing His inner spiritual nature. Grief was something thrust upon our Lord by His opposition. It was flung at Him along with blows and curses. He did not exchange His joy for sorrow; the sorrow came from without. The joy remained within. All the hostility that built up against Him, all the conspiring that resulted in His betrayal, arrest, imprisonment, trial, conviction, sentencing, flogging, and crucifixion, did not change Jesus. If He became acquainted with grief, it was only to endure it.

Perhaps it has occurred to you to question why the figure of our Savior is so seldom depicted with a benign or joyful expression on His face. Traditionally He appears solemn and sad, and often in a state of extreme agony, both in sculpture and on canvas. For centuries the principal representation of our Lord that the world has known is a man hanging on a cross. It should be remembered that as horrible as the crucifixion was, and as momentous for our salvation as it proved to be, it was followed by the resurrection, in which the heavenly Father turned death and seeming defeat and despair into glorious victory. That victory is still being celebrated by followers of The Way, not only at the Easter season but every day of the calendar year.

Rather than pursue this subject further, I prefer to translate a sonnet, "On the Resurrection," written by Tommaso Campanella (1568-1639), an Italian poet and philosopher. This man began his career as a Dominican monk, but spent twenty-six years in a Naples prison for his political and religious views. Here is his sonnet, written in the form of a question:[6]

> If Christ remained but six hours on the cross
> after a few years of sorrow and affliction,
> which He suffered willingly for humankind
> that Heaven might be purchased forever,
> why is He everywhere to be seen
> painted and preached only in torments

which were light compared with the joy
    that followed
when the wicked world's cruel blows were finished?

Why not talk and write about the majestic Kingdom
He enjoys in Heaven and soon will bring to earth
to the glory and praise of His worthy name?
O foolish crowd, because you are so earthbound
and have eyes only for the day of His ordeal,
you see His high triumph shorn of its true worth.

James, the brother of Jesus, begins his letter in the New Testament by advising his fellow Christians:

> Consider it pure joy, my brothers, whenever you face trials of many kinds, because you know that the testing of your faith develops perseverance. Perseverance must finish its work so that you may be mature and complete, not lacking anything.[7]

Peter adopts the same tone in his letter:

> Dear friends, do not be surprised at the painful trial you are suffering, as though something strange were happening to you. But rejoice [be filled with joy] that you participate in the sufferings of Christ, so that you may be overjoyed when his glory is revealed.[8]

Because this book is devoted to joy rather than suffering, we do not dwell on Jesus' various confrontations with His enemies among the religious leadership; nor will we describe what He underwent during the closing days of His ministry in Jerusalem. The disappointments, the loss of support, the anguish, the pain of torture, the agony of separation from His Father, all have been treated at length by persons better qualified than I. We shall probably never know the depths to which our Lord descended until we "see Him as He is."[9]

There is no need to apologize for this omission. Far more books have been written about the sufferings of Jesus than about His joy. In the same way, I am not attempting to "explain" or "account for" the meaning of suffering in the life of humanity. Every day I am committed to pray for loved ones who are in distress or acute physical pain. We all know individuals for whom life is anything but a joyride. To suggest that this book is a "how to" remedy for the afflictions of humankind is to do a cruel service to those afflicted.

Oswald Chambers points out that Jesus despised the shame of the cross because of the joy set before Him, Chambers making clear that it was not the cross Jesus despised, but the shame.[10] The distinction is important.

Today we are seeing a small improvement in the attitude our generation is taking toward disabled and handicapped persons, and thankfully we are learning to despise not the "shame" of being handicapped, but the shame many people have associated with it. By accepting the reality of the problem, we are better able to help. As Chambers says, God can take any person and put the miracle of His joy into him, and enable that person to manifest it in the actual details of life.

In other words, the joy is not blotted out by adversity; it simply waits until the cloud passes. It does not deny the existence of the cloud; it does not despise the cloud, or fight it. It waits, knowing that when at long last the sky clears, the joy will shine brighter than ever.

What Peter and James are conveying to us in their letters, as I understand it, is that suffering is not to be reached for, to be sought actively as something desirable. Pain after all is not a joyous thing and never was. What they are saying is that when it comes, we should not be surprised. Jesus went through it; why should we expect to be exempt?

But let me add a warning here. Jesus did not have a martyr complex; that is, He was not a pathological martyr in the sense that He simply could not wait to undergo pain and suffering. Traces of such behavior can be found in the history of the early church, but not in Jesus.

He did say that He had a baptism to be baptized with, "and how distressed I am [or straitened—pressed in] till it be accomplished,"[11] but that reference was to the vocation of His whole life which He had received from His Father. What He obviously wanted was to get through it so He could return to the joy of His Father's presence.

The church has never represented Jesus as dying on the cross with a fixed grin on His face. What He suffered, He suffered, and the Scripture tells us that He learned obedience through His sufferings.[12]

When James tells his fellow Christians they are to esteem it joy when they find themselves in situations that test their faith, he is telling them that certain kinds of suffering do in fact build fiber into our souls and strengthen our characters. When we pass through such a test, we are better men and women, which is cause for joy. James is not saying we should take delight simply in being hurt.

Peter, when he speaks of the "fiery trial" being experienced by some Christians "among you," is obviously referring to the suffering created by a current wave of persecution. He helps them to see that in a sense they are sharing the sufferings of Christ, which is a cause for joy.[13] The apostle Paul in the same vein writes to the Philippians about the "fellowship of His [that is, of Christ's] sufferings."[14] He tells the Corinthians that such suffering is cause for encouragement.[15] And to the Romans he declares that the sufferings of the present are not worth comparing to the glory that is soon to be revealed.[16]

In all this the New Testament never attempts to mix suffering with joy. The two are as separate as they are in the thirtieth Psalm, which says:

> Weeping may endure for a night,
>   but joy comes in the morning.[17]

That is because joy is an attribute of God, a thing apart, a wonderful sense of elation and exuberance in which tears and grief play no part. It is Jesus' secret, which He carried with Him all the way through His ordeal, and which burst again into full bloom at the resurrection.

Is there then no joy in pain, not even at the "higher levels of consciousness"? I don't know. Pain and I are not strangers, but there are regions into which it would be wise for me not to enter. Rather let me share what a friend told me about her experience in jail. I will omit all details except to say that during the events that led to her being incarcerated in the ladies' section of the county correctional center, she suffered excruciating pain.

My friend is a Christian, but as she lay on the steel bunk in her cell, her mood was definitely not one of joy and gladness. She did not regret the stand she had taken on a particular ethical issue, but she paid a heavy price. Both her shoulders were dislocated. In the midst of her suffering, the young woman who was her cell-mate approached her bunk. She was crying, and she said, "I'm so sorry to bother you, I know you're hurting, but you see I've just got to know Jesus and get right with God. I've been horrible. Please, please tell me how to find God!"

"At that moment," says my friend, "I knew pain, but I also knew joy."

Perhaps you are asking, "Where is the 'takeaway' in all this for me? Is there something I can do if I want to get in on Jesus' secret?" Yes, there is. For openers, go to a Christian bookstore and get yourself a brand new Bible. Start reading in both the Old and New Testaments, underlining such words as joy, delight, gladness and singing wherever you come across them.

Take special note of the last three verses of the book of the prophet Habakkuk, who was one of the greatest men of any age. He wrote at the time of Nebuchadnezzar's conquest of Jerusalem (586 B.C.) and his words apply directly to us in the 1990s:

> Though the fig tree does not bud
>   and there are no grapes on the vines
> though the olive crop fails
>   and the fields produce no food,
> though there are no sheep in the pen
>   and no cattle in the stalls,
> yet will I revel in the LORD,
>   I will shout for joy in the God of my salvation.
> The Lord God is my strength
>   and he makes my feet like hinds' feet
> as I walk upon the high places.[18]

What contentment! What deep assurance! The promise is that even when life's supports fail us, our faith in God has us walking on air—light-hearted and sure-footed.

I suggest you make a resolution not to dwell unduly on the one problem that is giving you so much trouble. Shelve it for the moment. Strip off the soiled garments of self-pity, put on the clean linen of a cheerful countenance, and start looking around. We were not placed here to help ourselves, but to serve the Lord and help each other. Try echoing the words of the psalmist who said, "Let me hear joy and gladness!"[19]

Start making your own music. You'll find there are plenty of words to go with it. One more time from Jeremiah:

> When your words came, I ate them;
>   they were my joy and my heart's delight.[20]

ⓞⓞⓞ

➤*Questions for Discussion*

1. In what way was Jesus a Man of Sorrows and in what way was He a Man of Joy?

2. What does Scripture mean when it says (Hebrews 12:2) that Jesus despised the shame of the cross, rather than the cross itself?

3. How can we maintain a feeling of joy when we are plunged into severe difficulty?

15

Place of Joy

*If you think Heaven will be boring,
you may have it mixed up
with a different spot.*

A Christian gentleman died full of years and went to Heaven where, according to the way these stories go, he was greeted by the apostle Peter. After inviting the newcomer through the gates, Peter supposedly asked him what he would like to do.

"Well," said the man, "I used to sing in my church choir, and I also sang with Cliff Barrows at the Billy Graham crusades. I'd like to join the choir up here if I could."

"Of course you can," replied Peter. "Right now they're over at the amphitheater rehearsing with Archangel Gabriel. Why don't you join them?"

So the man followed the suggestion, and as he later told his friends, "It was a most astonishing sight. There were a thousand sopranos, and a thousand altos, and a thousand basses, and I was the only tenor!"

He took his seat in his section and joined in as they practiced the songs of Zion and Moses and the Lamb. He was having a glorious time until Gabriel paused and rapped with his baton. Said Gabriel, "May we have a little less tenor, please?"

Stories about Heaven are legend, and many of them are spiced with humor, but wishful thinking is the source of most of them. Millions of people do not realize that there is an authentic source of information about Heaven, supported by the highest possible authority. This source tells us that the most important fact about Heaven is that it is a place of great zest and exhilarating joy.

Since our book is about joy, we shall spend this final chapter investigating the Bible's teaching about the joys of Heaven. As is well known, the Bible has a great deal to say about the end of history, about wrath and judgment and hell. It utters terrible warnings to evildoers and unbelievers who take the way that leads to destruction. But the Bible also has a great deal to say about Heaven, and since Christians fully expect to be delivered from judgment by the mercy and grace of Jesus Christ, they naturally turn with anticipation to the entrancing subject of life in Heaven.

The closing chapters of the Book of Revelation provide us with an unparalleled picture of Heaven as the Holy Spirit manifested it to John. The whole vision of John in the Apocalypse is a work of such beauty and magnificence that it takes one's breath away. It leaves me personally groping for words that do not come.

Nevertheless I am committed to a fresh discovery of the joy that Jesus Christ, the Man of joy, has brought to earth, and which He promised was only a foretaste of Heaven. And as I gaze about this tired old planet of ours, and see how many people are trapped in a joyless kind of existence, without seasoning, savor or hope, I cannot help looking beyond the edge of life itself. I want to know if it is true that Heaven is where everything comes right.

Like yourself perhaps, I am aware of friends for whom this life has not been a very enjoyable excursion. I have walked the wards as a hospital chaplain. I have sat at the bedside of war veterans and looked at their broken bodies and wasted limbs. I have worked with retarded children. As a pastor I have prayed with the dying. I am not unaware of the sufferings of the handicapped, the bereaved, or the victims of severe depression and dread disease.

But the promise of the Word of God is that Heaven is going to be different. Because he has taken Jesus Christ into his heart and has made Him Lord of his life, that young enlisted man who, because of a combat wound, is today bound to a wheelchair for life, will some day have a new body. That diabetic child will one day be healed and freed from insulin. That woman who has agonized with pain in bed most of her life will become hale and hearty. That doomed child of a drug addict will be running and leaping in the full bloom of health. That truck driver lying in a coma as a result of a freeway tragedy will find himself awake and shouting for joy. That victim of a rapist or wife abuser will be enraptured to find she has no humiliating feelings or memories to cloud her mind; that person who suffered so many years with chemical imbalance and emotional bondage will be restored to sound health, free from pills forever; that prey of a drive-by shooting will be given a resurrection body that is clean and strong and beautiful.

And how will all this transpire? By faith. By simple trust in the Messiah, the Son of God, the Savior of the world, who loved us and gave Himself for us. And where will it all happen? In Heaven. Perhaps now we should take a closer look at John's vision, to see what Heaven will be like—and what it will not be like.

The first and paramount experience in Heaven will be seeing the face of Jesus. My word processor would burn up if I tried to describe that. John says explicitly, "They will see His face."[1] That alone, for millions of Christians from every walk of life, will be Heaven.

But there is much more. Heaven will not be issuing us harps and ordering up fleecy clouds for us to sit on and twang away for a millennium or two. That is a travesty of Heaven; in fact, if Heaven were like that, 99 percent of Christians would prefer to be somewhere else. Take this for an absolute fact: No one will be bored in Heaven. How do I know? Because God will be there. "The dwelling of God is with men, and he will live with them. They will be his people, and God himself will be with them and be their God."[2] I know it because God's Word tells me that Heaven is a place of eternal joy, where goodness, truth and beauty prevail.

There will be magnificent scenery. In his vision John gives us just a hint of a great river, with groves of the Tree of Life bordering the stream and the broad streets of a city bustling with activity and social life. "And the leaves of the tree are for the healing of the nations."[3] The place will be alive with color—color which many of our blind Christian friends will see for the first time, and will enjoy and revel in. The nations from all the continents will be represented there, each resplendent in dignity and honor. Royalty will be present. Blacks, whites, browns, reds, yellows, all hues of color will mix together joyfully. The curse is lifted, and in Christ they are true brothers and sisters at last.

John tells us that the old order of things will have passed away when we get to Heaven. There will be no more death or mourning or crying or pain. Doors will presumably have no locks, for crime will be unknown; all the crooks will be reborn or be somewhere else. Time will mean nothing; we shall be contemporaries with the great ones of history, with Noah and Moses and Deborah and Esther and Mary and Stephen and Paul and Peter and all the rest.

Even more wonderful, there are hints that we shall be reunited with our loved ones who trust the Lord. It's even possible we may meet the grandparents we never knew. Think about it!

And the celebrating! Imagine what it will be like when all we have to do is praise the Lord and do His bidding. Just what our activity will entail is not clear: "It has not yet been revealed what we shall be."[4] But try to imagine all the ingenuity of the human mind, set to work in creative achievements! For some of us it will mean perhaps doing the kind of fulfilling and challenging thing we always wanted to do, but never got to do on earth. What a blast!

Some of the older Bible commentaries distinguish between what they call "spiritual" and "carnal" activities, and assure us that we shall all be very religious when we get to Heaven, and do very religious things. I think the distinction is overdrawn. We will not be invisible, according to the Scripture, nor will we be angels, but we will have resurrection bodies. We will be human beings, just as Moses and Elijah were human beings on the Mount of Transfiguration.[5] The nature of our heavenly bodies is not fully spelled out, but if you understand that Heaven is not peopled with spooks or disembodied spirits, but with live heavenly bodies that are filled with joy and delight, I think you will arrive at some idea of the wonderful times with Jesus, the Man of Joy, that lie ahead.

> And only The Master shall praise us,
>   and only The Master shall blame;
> And no one shall work for money,
>   and no one shall work for fame,
> But each for the joy of the working,
>   and each, in his separate star,
> Shall draw the Thing as he sees It
>   for the God of Things as they are.[6]

John tells us in his vision, "The throne of God and of the Lamb will be in the city, and his servants will serve him."[7] When Jesus was asked the question about marriage in Heaven, He replied that after the resurrection those who had risen would be "like the angels."[8] They would be *like* the angels, but they would not *be* angels. The New Testament describes some important similarities and dissimilarities in Heaven between angels and saints (the saints being redeemed and resurrected sinners).

In his book, *Angels: God's Secret Agents,* Billy Graham points out that angels carry messages. If you look carefully at the word *evangelist*, you will find the root word *angel* implanted in it. Angel comes from a common Greek word *angelos* meaning "messenger" or "one sent." In ancient Greek literature an angel was always a messenger, whether human or supernatural.

That gives us a clue to the way we shall serve the Lord when we get to Heaven. It will be a time of sheer joy. Jesus, you remember, said that in the courts of Heaven we would be like the angels; and since angels are messengers by definition, we can reasonably expect to be sent on missions wherever God in His wisdom chooses to send us. Does that sound boring?

I talked with Gordon Cooper, one of the original seven American astronauts, after he had made his second orbital flight around the earth in a spacecraft. Colonel Cooper is a Christian. As he described his voyage in the Gemini 5 some 150 miles above the earth, it didn't sound very boring to me. If you think Heaven will be boring, you may have it mixed up with a different spot.

The "city" John refers to is the New Jerusalem, the Holy City which he saw in his vision. John said it was coming down out of Heaven from God (he said it was a "new heaven"),[9] and he thereby opened a discussion that has been going on for two thousand years. Is the Holy City as John visioned it "coming down out of heaven" an actual description of Heaven or not? And if not, where is Heaven?

As far as the future of believers is concerned, there is really no argument, because to us God and Heaven are the same. If God dwells in the Holy City—and John says He does—that is enough. Call it whatever you choose; call it Utopia if you wish. I shall call it Heaven.

We will now turn our attention to another matter, and attempt to learn how, after this life is over, we can arrive at that place of blissfulness we have been discussing. We wish to be certain that once the coroner has established the unalterable fact that we are no longer among the living creatures of earth, we will proceed expeditiously, safely, surely, and directly to our desired goal.

The operant word is "Jesus." The Bible tells us that He is the key, the door, the gateway to paradisaical realms. He Himself assured us that Heaven was a real place and that we would all be welcome, that there was plenty of room, and that first class accommodations awaited us upon our arrival. If it be true, then, that joy is the business of Heaven, that alone ought to be incentive enough to draw most of the population of this planet to seek it, regardless of the religion in which an individual was reared.

But how do we get there? And how do we know for certain that Jesus was speaking truly when He said we will be welcome when we do get there? Isn't there another place to which some people go when they die—a place not quite so attractive? Just because everyone is invited to this bourne of everlasting joy, does that mean everyone will automatically enter?

Because these questions are on the minds of many people, let us try to answer the direct question, How do we get there?

One way to approach a reply is for us to think of our making a journey to a foreign country. What do we need? First we need transportation, and that requires a ticket. A ticket is a written pledge that guarantees the journey. Scripture tells us, "If you confess with your mouth, 'Jesus is Lord,' and believe in your heart that God raised him from the dead, you will be saved."[10] Jesus Himself said, "Whoever hears my word and believes him who sent me has eternal life, and will not be condemned; he has crossed over from death to life."[11]

So much for the ticket. How about a passport? Scripture says:

> Nothing impure will ever enter it [Heaven], nor will anyone who does what is shameful or deceitful, but only those whose names are written in the Lamb's book of life.[12]

Our name in the book: That is our passport.

Will we have to pass immigration? All we need is a longing for a better country, a heavenly one.[13] What about vaccination and inoculation? No problem. With no ill-nesses, aches or pains, there will be no injections. "[God will] wipe every tear from their eyes."[14]

Do we need luggage? What about clothing? We need to take nothing. "We brought nothing into this world, and we can take nothing out of it."[15] As for clothing, a complete new wardrobe ("garments of salvation") is to be provided for each new arrival.[16]

Currency, perhaps? Yes! "Store up for yourselves treasures in heaven, where moth and rust do not destroy, and where thieves do not break in and steal."[17]

Will there be time changes? No. Resetting of watches will not be necessary. Nor will the watches. There is no night there.[18] There are no time zones. There is no time.

Will there be customs, and what will we need to declare? We need to declare the Gospel that "Christ died for our sins according to the Scriptures, and that he was buried, and that he rose again."[19]

When and where do we make reservations? Immedi-ately, at the house of God. Booking is open. "Now is the time of God's favor, now is the day of salvation."[20]

What will be our departure time? "It is not for you to know the times or dates the Father has set by his own authority."[21]

How will we know when we get there? A coronation ceremony is arranged for each brother and sister on arrival—"a crown of righteousness, which the Lord, the righteous Judge, will award . . . on that day . . . to all who have longed for his appearing."[22]

So there it is. God offers us inner joy here on earth and forever after through Jesus Christ. Do we have it? I don't mean happiness. Happiness has been defined as the look on a dieter's face on reaching the desired weight and heading for a restaurant. Inner joy is something different. It's there between meals. It comes "trailing clouds of glory."[23] It has springs deep down inside. Billy Sunday once declared, "If you have no joy, there's a leak in your Christianity somewhere."[24] Jesus gives that joy. I repeat, do we have it? If we don't, let's go for it. Let's "get in the flow." What is holding us back? Our sins? There is the cross: Come, kneel. Unload them! There is grace: Take it! Tune in to the heavenly symphony that the poet Dante says he heard when he came to Paradise:[25]

> All Heaven broke forth, "Be glory!" Such
>   sweet din . . .
> And all I saw, meseemed to see therein
> A smile of all creation.

If Dante could see smiles and hear music in the turning of the "great wheels" of the universe,[26] you and I ought to reach out right now and find some joy in our lives. As Robert Louis Stevenson reminded us, "To miss the joy is to miss all."[27] It's there! We don't need to wait for Heaven. And when we do find the inner joy that Jesus brought, let's not keep it to ourselves. Let's sing and shout it.

I have one other request to make. When you find the inner joy that was Jesus' secret, will you take it with you to church? Our churches need revival. They need a fresh filling of the Holy Spirit that will bring back the gladness of heart they once knew. There are such wonderful people in our churches. They believe, they pray, they love—but they

worry. You make them feel the blessing. Open your Bible
and read them a psalm:

> Shout for joy to the LORD, all the earth.
>   Serve the LORD with gladness;
>   come before him with joyful songs.[28]

○○○

➤ *Questions for Discussion*

1. What grounds do Christians have for believing that
   Heaven is more than a fantasy in people's minds?

2. How will believers differ from angels in Heaven?

3. If you found yourself in Heaven tomorrow, who or
   what would you look for?

Reference Notes

Chapter 1 - The Secret

1. Alfred Tennyson, "In Memoriam."
2. San Francisco Chronicle, July 13, 1990.

Chapter 2 - Cosmic Joy

1. Luke 10:21.
2. Luke 1:35; Matthew 1:21.
3. Genesis 1:1,2.
4. Cf. Umberto Cassuto, Commentary on the Book of Genesis, Part One, tr. by I. Abrahams (Jerusalem: The Magnes Press (Hebrew University), 1961), pp. 24-25.
5. Keil & Delitzsch, Commentary on the Old Testament, vol. 1, tr. by James Martin (Grand Rapids: Eerdmans, 1986), p. 49.
6. Psalm 19:1, NKJV.
7. See chapter 15.
8. Luke 12:32, NKJV.
9. Isaiah 65:18.
10. Zephaniah 3:17.
11. Joseph Addison, "Ode" in The Spectator (1712 A.D.).
12. In 1962 Major Andrian G. Nikolayev, a Soviet cosmonaut, made a space flight in the Vostok III that successfully orbited the earth. On his return to Russian soil Major Nikolayev was quoted as saying that he "didn't see any God up there." But as many have since remarked, God saw him. For further word of the universe creating music, see chapter 15, note 26.
13. Nehemiah 8:10.

Chapter 3 - Laughter

1. No date or translator is mentioned. The original Italian version is also in the Library of Congress.
2. Romans 14:17.
3. Jeremiah 7:34; Proverbs 15:15, 17:22; Psalms 126:2, 43:4; Isaiah 49:13; Jeremiah 33:11, NKJV; John 16:20,22; 1 Peter 1:8, NIV.
4. Luke 10:17.
5. Hebrews 12:2.
6. Cf. Matthew 6:25,26.
7. John Knox, The Man Christ Jesus (Chicago: Willett & Clark, 1942), pp. 56-59.
8. Matthew 28:8, NKJV.
9. Carl F. H. Henry, "The Significance of the Resurrection" in Spiritual Witness, ed. S. E. Wirt (Wheaton, IL: Crossway, 1991), chapter 10.
10. G. K. Chesterton, Orthodoxy (Garden City, NY: Image Books, Doubleday, 1959), p. 160.
11. Eugene O'Neill, Lazarus Laughed (New York: Boni & Liveright, 1927), act 1, scene 1.
12. John 11:43,44.
13. C. S. Lewis, Surprised by Joy (New York: Harcourt, Brace, 1956), p. 238.
14. Richard Rolle (c. 1295-1349), "The Fire of Love," from De Incendio Amoris, tr. from Latin in 1435 by Richard Misyn, ed. by Ralph Harvey (London: Kegan Paul, 1896), pp. 50-51.
15. Cal Samra, The Joyful Christ (San Francisco: Harper & Row, 1986).

Chapter 4 - Religious Smog

1. John 10:10.
2. "D. W. Harvey lists thirteen Hebrew roots and twenty-seven separate words for joy or joyful." —International Standard Biblical Encyclopedia (Grand Rapids: Eerdmans, 1982), 2:1140.
3. Psalms 100:1; 150:5; 150:4; 49:3; 148:3; 147:12; 28:7; 63:4; 65:12; 65:13.
4. Isaiah 49:13, 60:15; Nehemiah 8:10; Zephaniah 3:17; Ecclesiastes 2:26 (NKJV.)
5. Psalm 98:8, Isaiah 55:12.
6. Decision magazine, October 1968. Used by permission.
7. Cf. Matthew 18:20.
8. Interview on May 7, 1963, published inter alia in God in the Dock, Essays on Theology and Ethics, by C. S. Lewis (Grand Rapids: Eerdmans, 1970), p. 259.
9. Dudley Zuver, Salvation by Laughter (New York: Harper & Brothers, 1933), p. 260.
10. The Elisabeth Elliot Newsletter, Ann Arbor, July/August 1990, p. 3.
11. Ed Wheat, M.D., Love Life for Every Married Couple (Grand Rapids: Zondervan, 1989), p. 12.
12. Samuel Chadwick, The Way to Pentecost (Fort Washington, PA: Christian Literature Crusade, 1976), pp. 35-36.
13. Acts 13:52.

Chapter 5 - Enjoying Him Forever

1. Cf. John 2:1ff.
2. Cf. Hebrews 1:9.
3. Isaiah 53:3, NKJV.

4. Research has revealed a multiplicity of versions of "The Ballad of Casey Jones." The one I learned (and tried to sing) as a boy in Berkeley, California, began with the line, "It's a long hard run from Lynchburg to Danville." For another version, see "The American Songbag," ed., Carl Sandburg (New York: Harcourt, Brace & World, 1927), p. 336.

5. Hebrews 12:2, NKJV.

6. Mark 10:13-16.

7. Fyodor Dostoevsky, TheBrothers Karamazov, tr., Constance Garnett (New York: Modern Library, n.d.), p. 379.

8. John 2:5.

9. Cf. John 2:9,10.

10. All the recent translations have discarded "shed abroad" in favor of "poured out," which is the better rendition of the Greek (ekkechutai). Cf. Romans 5:5. See also Alford's Greek Testament (Grand Rapids: Baker Book House, 1980), 2:357.

Chapter 6 - 'Pecooler Noshuns'

1. Matthew 23:24; Mark 10:25; Luke 11:39; Matthew 12:26-28; 7:6; Luke 6:39; Matthew 8:22; Luke 6:44; 8:16; Matthew 7:3-5.

2. Matthew 19:13.

3. William Barclay, The Gospel of Mark (Daily Study Bible) (Edinburgh: Saint Andrew Press), p. 40.

4. Mark 2:1-12.

5. Cf. Matthew 15:21-28.

6. Topical Encyclopedia of Living Quotations (Minneapolis: Bethany House, 1982), no. 1578.

7. D. Elton Trueblood, The Humor of Christ (New York: Harper & Row, 1964).

8. Luke 7:34; 7:18-28; Matthew 12:1-4; 1 Samuel 21:1-6.

9. Mark 1:16-20.

10. Cf. Mark 2:14.

11. Topical Encyclopedia, no. 1139.

12. Ibid, no. 1137.

13. Emil Brunner, The Theology of Crisis (New York: Scribners, 1930), p. 54.

14. Cf. 1 Corinthians 15:6.

Chapter 7 - Beatitudes

1. Matthew 5:3-10.

2. The Cross on the Mountain: The Beatitudes in the Light of the Cross (New York: Thomas Y. Crowell, 1959).

3. William Barclay, "The Gospel of Matthew," The Daily Study Bible, vol. 1 (Edin-

burgh: The Saint Andrew Press, 1962), pp. 83-85.

4. Gerhard Kittel, et al., Theological Dictionary of the New Testament, tr. and abridged by Geoffrey W. Bromiley (Grand Rapids: Eerdmans, 1985), p. 548.

5. Luke 1:48.

6. Jude 24.

7. Matthew 5:3.

8. Luke 6:20, NKJV.

9. Galatians 5:22.

10. Cf. Ephesians 4:13.

11. Irenaeus is quoted by John Powell, S. J. in Joan Winmill Brown, Joy in His Presence (Minneapolis: World Wide Publications, 1982), entry for October 12.

12. Luke 18:13, NKJV.

13. 2 Corinthians 4:7, NKJV.

Chapter 8 - The Ultimate

1. Quoted in Gerald Kennedy, The Lion and the Lamb (Nashville: Abingdon-Cokesbury, 1950), p. 85.

2. "Heureux les débonnaires, car ils heriteront de la terre."

3. Luke 6:38.

4. This ballad by Ernest Lawrence Thayer (1863-1940) was first published in the San Francisco Examiner, June 3, 1888.

5. D. Elton Trueblood, The Humor of Christ (San Francisco: Harper & Row, 1989), p. 32. Cf. Ephesians 1:10.

6. John 20:20.

7. Cf. Acts 12:1-16.

8. Gordon W. Allport, Personality, a Psychological Interpretation (London: Constable, 1949), pp. 224-25.

9 Romans 14:17; 15:13; Galatians 5:22; John 15:10,11; 1 John 1:4.

Chapter 9 - Celebrate!

1. Robert Louis Stevenson, Underwoods Book I: The Celestial Surgeon (lyrical poems, pub. in 1887).

2. Luke 10:20; John 16:22; Romans 5:2; Philippians 1:18; 3:1; 4:4; Luke 19:37.

3. Deuteronomy 26:11; 1 Chronicles 16:10; Psalms 68:3; 85:6; 89:15,16; 96:11,12; 98:4; 105:43; 119:14; Proverbs 5:18; 29:2; 28:12; Isaiah 29:19; Jeremiah 32:41; Zephaniah 3:17.

4. Title of a noteworthy sermon preached by the Rev. Jonathan Edwards in Northampton, Massachusetts, in 1741.

5. Isaiah 56:7.

6. Mark 14:28.

7. John 21:12,13.

Chapter 10 - Parables

1. Mark 3:23.
2. Gerhard, Kittel et al., *Theological Dictionary of the New Testament*, abridged, tr. by Geoffrey W. Bromiley (Grand Rapids: Eerdmans, 1985), p. 774.
3. Luke 15:3-32.
4. John 6:38.
5. Matthew 9:15; Mark 2:19; Luke 5:34.
6. Cf. Isaiah 62:5; John 3:29; Revelation 21:2; 22:17.
7. Matthew 25:14-23. The NIV paraphrases verse 23 as "Come and share your master's happiness." The Greek text, however, clearly refers to the Kingdom: *eiselthé* (enter into) *ten charan* (the joy) *tou kuriou sou* (of your Lord).
8. Cf. Hebrews 12:2; 1 Corinthians 15:26.

Chapter 11 - The Expedition

1. John 9:1-9.
2. Luke 7:16, NKJV.
3. Luke 8:1, NKJV.
4. Matthew 8:16.
5. Luke 18:43.
6. Luke 13:17.
7. Mark 12:37, NKJV.
8. Matthew 7:21; John 5:30; 9:4.
9. John 15:11.
10. John 16:22.
11. Luke 24:13-34. The Emmaus walk is also mentioned in Mark 16:12.
12. Luke 24:25. The Greek word translated "fools" in the King James Version *(anoetoi)* means "not understanding."
13. Luke 24:32.
14. John 20:20.
15. Luke 24:42,43.
16. Acts 1:10, NKJV.
17. Cf. Henry Alford, *Alford's Greek Testament* (Grand Rapids: Baker Book House, 1980), 1:675.
18. Luke 24:51-53.
19. Cf. Acts 2:13.
20. Acts 2:14-21; cf. Joel 2:28-32.
21. The expression is taken from Milton's *Il Penseroso.*
22. Acts 2:26,28; cf. Psalm 16:9,11.
23. Acts 2:46,47.
24. Acts 2:47.
25. Acts 8:8.
26. Acts 8:39, NKJV.
27. Acts 13:52.
28. Acts 14:17.
29. Acts 16:34.
30. Acts 16:35-40.
31. Cf. Acts 27:34-37.
32. Acts 28:3-6.
33. Acts 28:15.
34. 2 Corinthians 4:8-10; 6:10; 7:4.
35. Acts 15:3.

Chapter 12 - Poets and Prophets

1. Isaiah 12:2,3; 35:1,2,10; 60:15; 61:1-3,7; 65:18, NIV and NKJV.
2. Proverbs 12:22; 15:15; 17:22; 21:15; 28:12; 23:24; 27:9.
3. Proverbs 8:30,31.
4. Jeremiah 15:16; 9:24.
5. Jeremiah 31:11-13.
6. Franz Delitzsch, "Commentary on the Song of Songs," tr. by M. G. Easton, p. 1, in Keil and Delitzsch, *Commentary on the Old Testament*, vol.6 (Grand Rapids: Eerdmans, 1986).
7. Ibid, pp. 7, 15.
8. Cf. David and Carol Hocking, *Romantic Lovers* (Eugene, OR: Harvest House, 1986); Ed Wheat, M.D., *Love Life for Every Married Couple* (Grand Rapids: Zondervan, 1980).
9. Delitzsch, op.cit., p.2.
10. Hengstenberg, Ernst, in R. A. Redford, "Introduction to the Exposition of the Song of Solomon," in *Pulpit Commentary* 9:xiv (Grand Rapids: Eerdmans, 1950).
11. Song of Songs, 2:1,4.
12. Wheat, op.cit., p. 155.
13. Song of Songs 7:6; 2:14; 4:9.
14. Redford, op.cit., in *Pulpit Commentary* 9:viii.
15. Matthew 12:34.
16. Hugh T. Kerr, Jr., "Exposition of The Song of Songs," *The Interpreter's Bible* (Nashville: Abingdon, 1980), 5:132.
17. Acts 3:21.
18. Revelation 21:2.
19. Song of Songs 8:14.

Chapter 13 - Amazing Grace

1. Mark 1:15.
2. John 10:18.
3. 2 Corinthians 5:19, NKJV.
4. R. A. Torrey, *Questions Answered* (Chicago: Moody Press, 1909), p. 9.
5. A. J. Gossip, "Exposition of the Gospel According to St. John," *The Interpreter's Bible* (Nashville: Abingdon, 1980), 8:770-71.
6. Robert Browning's poem, "Bishop Blougram's Apology."

Chapter 14 - 'Man of Sorrows'

1. 1 Peter 1:6.

2. Mark 1:13.
3. Mark 2:1-5.
4. Mark 2:15; 3:1ff.
5. Mark 3:6.
6. This rendition differs slightly from a nineteenth century English translation by John Addington Symonds (1840-1893). I wish to thank Mr. Phil Palermo for his kind assistance. In its present form the poem was published in a collection titled *The Country of the Risen King*, Merle Meeter, ed. (Grand Rapids: Baker Book House, 1978).
7. James 1:2-4.
8. 1 Peter 4:12,13.
9. 1 John 3:2.
10. *Oswald Chambers, The Best From All His Works, vol. 2*, Harry Verploegh, ed. (Nashville: Thomas Nelson, 1989), p. 162.
11. Luke 12:50, NKJV.
12. Hebrews 5:8.
13. 1 Peter 4:13.
14. Philippians 3:10.
15. 2 Corinthians 1:5.
16. Romans 8:18.
17. Psalm 30:5, NKLV
18. Habakkuk 3:17-19.
19. Psalm 51:8.
20. Jeremiah 15:16, NKJV.

Chapter 15 - Place of Joy

1. Revelation 22:4.
2. Revelation 21:3.
3. Revelation 22:2.
4. 1 John 3:2, NKJV.
5. Mark 9:2-8.
6. Rudyard Kipling, *L'Envoi*.
7. Revelation 22:3.
8. Mark 12:25, NKJV.
9. Revelation 21:1,2.
10. Romans 10:9.
11. John 5:24.
12. Revelation 21:27.
13. Hebrews 11:16, NKJV.
14. Revelation 21:4.
15. 1 Timothy 6:7.
16. Isaiah 61:10.
17. Matthew 6:20.
18. Revelation 21:25.
19. 1 Corinthians 15:3,4, NKJV.
20. 2 Corinthians 6:2.
21. Acts 1:7.
22. 2 Timothy 4:8.
23. William Wordsworth: Ode, *Intimations of Immortality*.

24. Frank S. Mead, editor, *Encyclopedia of Religious Quotations* (Westwood, N.J.: Revell, 1965), p. 259.
25. *The Comedy of Dante Alighieri*, tr. by Dorothy L. Sayers and Barbara Reynolds, Cantica III, "Paradise," Canto 27 (Harmondsworth, England: Penguin, 1976), p. 291.
26. Ibid, pp. 55, 60-61. Cf Job 38:7: "The morning stars sang together and all the angels [sons of God] shouted for joy." Pythagoras, the Greek philosopher (c. 530 B.C.) is said to have taught that the stars emanated music as they revolved through the heavens. The same thought recurs in Cicero ("The Dream of Scipio") and in Shakespeare ("The Merchant of Venice," Act 5, Scene 1).
27. *Topical Encyclopedia of Living Quotations*, eds. Wirt and Beckstrom (Minneapolis: Bethany, 1982), No. 1818.
28. Psalm 100:1,2.

Index